SENIOR CYBER

Best Security Practices
for Your Golden Years

SCOTT N. SCHOBER
with Craig W. Schober

Senior Cyber: Best Security Practices for Your Golden Years

Copyright© 2021 Scott N. Schober and Craig W. Schober

Published by ScottSchober.com Publishing
Metuchen, New Jersey

Hardcover ISBN: 978-0-9969022-9-8
Paperback ISBN: 978-1-7363158-0-4
eISBN: 978-1-7363158-1-1

Cover and Interior Design by GKS Creative
Copyediting and Proofreading by Kimberly A. Bookless
Illustrations by Jake Thomas of Jake Thomas Creative
Project Management by The Cadence Group

This book may be purchased for educational, business, or sales promotional use. For information, please email info@scottschober.com, call 732-548-3737, or visit www.ScottSchober.com.

Dedicated to George (William) Schober. Beloved grandfather, pioneering inventor, and the original Senior Cyber.

Is not wisdom found among the aged,
and does not understanding
come with a long life?

Job 12:12

Contents

Introduction

This book is meant to be an encouraging, easy read for those of us who have lived through a slew of technological and social changes and want to manage successfully and safely in this new digital world. In fact, I cherish those readers, specifically, for their insight and wisdom that can come only from a lifetime of experience. I have also strived to inject some humor throughout the book, which is designed to help you navigate the ever-changing digital world of computers and the internet—also called cyberspace.

As the president and CEO of Berkeley Varitronics Systems (BVS), I have designed and sold thousands of cybersecurity products to small businesses, Fortune 500 companies, and the US government, so you might be wondering why a cybersecurity expert is writing a book directed toward senior citizens. In my first book, *Hacked Again: It Can Happen to Anyone . . . Even a Cybersecurity Expert*, I shared the details of my story about how I was targeted and repeatedly hacked. After that, I began to hear similar stories affecting not just individuals but also their businesses, employees, and customers. I quickly came to the conclusion that *Cybersecurity Is Everybody's Business,* which also served as the title of my second book.

All too often, I found myself preaching to the choir. I speak to thousands of people every year on a range of cybersecurity topics, but those audiences are primarily made up of chief executive officers (CEOs) and chief information security officers (CISOs) trying to protect their small businesses from an onslaught of increasing cyberthreats. These are the generals who send troops into the trenches; they don't have targets on their own backs.

Consumers, on the other hand, are routinely targeted and attacked by a variety of hackers, malware, and scammers. They don't have the protective high-tech information technology (IT) teams, sophisticated security software, or golden parachutes that corporate executives typically deploy when they are summarily ejected for failing to secure their own companies. Seniors, in particular, fall into this category, and I want to make sure you don't have to go through any of the negative experiences so many others have.

We all have the right to learn, forget things, make mistakes, and have a good laugh. Many seniors tend to shy away from things that are new and avoid anything that might appear to be related to the cyberworld, so I am purposely avoiding extended technical explanations. However, we cannot avoid the change and progression that comes with all technology, so

I have taken time to focus on practical steps all seniors can take to stay safe on the internet.

Let's face it: getting older stinks. Joints ache. Hearing fails. Hair loss becomes a daily occurrence. However, I will not throw in the towel so easily and give up on my senior readers. As I write this, I have just turned fifty, and, while not technically a senior, I am starting to realize I am not quite as invincible as I once thought I was. For example, I can no longer eat whatever I please. Apparently, my eyesight has been failing for years, and I just have begun to take notice of it. I could go into my bladder issues, but you've probably been there. In fact, you're probably a senior yourself or know one and are way ahead of me. I could easily go on and on about physical and mental challenges most seniors face; I see them in my parents' daily lives. They are in their midseventies and face their own set of technical and security challenges in addition to their unique medical demands.

Until this past year, my grandfather was alive and kicking for over ninety-nine years. We lost him just one month shy of his one-hundredth birthday, and what a fantastic mind he had right up until the end. I'll have much more to say about Bill Schober as a Cyber Senior model later in this book.

 SENIOR CYBER TIPS: Throughout the book, I will provide short, helpful takeaways and define some terms that might be unfamiliar under the term **SENIOR CYBER TIP** at the appropriate places in each chapter. Also note that the appendix of this book, entitled "Senior Scams and What to Look For," gives more specific visual information on how to spot the different types of scams you may encounter in your digital life. Feel free to share all this valuable information with anyone who needs it, because, while the cyberworld can be filled with wonders, it can also be dangerous if you don't know your way around it.

I hope *Senior Cyber* will empower all readers to take charge of your lives, cyber and otherwise. My goal is for you to remove any fear of computers, the internet, or cyberthieves. It's much better to embrace technology and enjoy its benefits rather than live in fear of it.

1

It's a Numbers Game

According to most studies, Americans in their forties have a median savings of $63,000. In their fifties, that number jumps to $117,000, and in their sixties, that number jumps up to $172,000.[1] The median savings number continues to rise for those aged seventy and beyond if they haven't significantly dipped into their retirement savings. This is great news for all thrifty seniors. Unfortunately,

---

1 Synchrony Staff, "What's the Median Retirement Savings by Age?" Synchrony Bank, March 30, 2020, https://www.synchronybank.com/blog/median-retirement-savings-by-age/.

criminals also know these statistics and act accordingly.

Cybercriminals and unscrupulous companies have targeted the elderly at an alarming rate. According to some 2018 estimates, fraud against the elderly has reached $36 billion per year.[2] That's more than a little chump change. In fact, seniors have moved up toward the top of most hackers' lists because, like most thieves, hackers generally target the easiest, most lucrative victims. While seniors have the advantage of wisdom and often have their guard up, they are also among the most vulnerable in society.

Most seniors are left out of the security conversation when it comes to technology, continuing education, and shoring up their cyberdefenses. Companies offer many security and privacy-based services to seniors, but they are typically in the form of alerts and fixes *after* the fact. Precious little is being done to

---

2   Robert Loh, "Elder Financial Abuse: A $36 Billion Opportunity for CFEs to Make a Difference," *Fraud Magazine,* November 2018, https://www.fraud-magazine.com/article.aspx?id=4295003889.

prevent fraud and theft. I also believe many of those types of offerings are somewhat patronizing and sometimes even predatory.

LOW-HANGING FRUIT

Surely you've seen a few recent headlines about the massive digital hacks of large retailers, including Target and Home Depot, and even financial institutions like JP Morgan Chase and Equifax. More than a quarter of all Fortune 500 companies have experienced security hacks over the past decade alone. These hacks can include stolen credit card information and other personal customer data; it's a wonder anyone trusts payment by credit card anymore. Don't get me wrong; the convenience of credit and debit cards has won even me over, but I have seen enough scams in my line of work to keep me on my toes. So if I can encourage just a few more credit card users to stay on their own toes, this book will be performing a valuable service to its readers.

Cash may still be king, but credit card use is on the rise, even though hundreds of millions of cards are stolen every year. The law of supply and demand doesn't stop for criminals, which is why you can find compromised credit cards—and just about anything else you can imagine—for sale on the Dark Web. You will probably never need to visit the Dark Web yourself, but like a conscientious neighbor, it's good to understand how the neighborhood works in case you ever need to help others navigate it.

 **SENIOR CYBER TIP:** The **Dark Web** is the part of the World Wide Web content *not* indexed by standard search engines, such

as Google or Bing. It is generally attributed
to hacking and illegal cyberactivity.

Due to the influx of so much stolen data
being bought, sold, and traded on the Dark
Web, the price of a stolen card is not what
it used to be. Criminals are always searching for the next big score, and many have
turned to senior citizens for an easy payday.
After all, seniors have lots of cash and little
experience with the latest technology. They
are natural targets, but they should not be
underestimated by anyone.

A MAGIC BULLET

I wish this book were enough, but truth be told, there is no magic bullet to stop the many threats to cybersecurity. The best prevention is education. A little education goes a long way, and more education goes much further than that. *Senior Cyber* is designed as a conversation starter as much as it is written to answer those nagging tech and security questions we all have from time to time.

I love teaching and presenting to all kinds of audiences, so even if this is the first—but not the last—book on cybersecurity you read, I hope you'll find it more interesting and informative than most of the other cybersecurity books out there. I don't wish to besmirch my fellow authors, but most books on this subject come across as potentially condescending, too complex, or just plain boring.

2

Technology Taken in Steps

Before we jump into security discussions involving the latest threats to modern smartphones, I want to step back for a moment to look at how the telephone has helped shape our relationship to technology.

The rotary telephone was invented in the late 1890s, and the first patent filed was by Almon Brown Strowger for a rotary dial on December 21, 1891. I fondly remember dialing our rotary phone in my home back in the early 1970s. I remember the sounds and the tactile sensations of dialing the precise number of a friend. I can even remember that I disliked phone numbers with many zeros because it seemed to take forever for the dial to circle back before I could dial in the next number. It's incredible how quickly we absorb, master, and then begin to resent that same technology.

Well, some things don't change, because Bell Telephone introduced the first phones featuring electronic push buttons and touch-tone dialing in late 1963. I guess rotary dials were just too slow for most, so my home, like many American homes, began to migrate over to the touch-tone variety. My kids scarcely understand the concept of a wall-mounted rotary phone in the home, but then again, I still have trouble grasping the complexities of the social media they seem to navigate so nimbly.

There were many more advancements to the basic phone over the next few decades. Fixed landline phones moved to cordless ones; cordless phones shifted to cellular; and cellular phones have leaped into our pockets and function as affordable supercomputers that can do almost anything. My point is that humans of all ages and backgrounds have the capacity to learn and even master technology when given the right motivations and a little help.

A VISION OF THE FUTURE

Pioneering scientist and inventor Nikola Tesla actually predicted similar progress in 1926. "When wireless is perfectly applied the whole earth will be converted into a huge brain," Tesla wrote. He continued, "We shall be able to communicate with one another instantly, irrespective of distance." Tesla sums up this mysterious future technology with: "A man will be able to carry one in his vest pocket."[3]

Sounds a lot like the internet and modern smartphones to me, but what Tesla couldn't have possibly predicted was the incredible array of services, apps (short for software applications),

---

3 Matt Novak, "Nikola Tesla's Incredible Predictions for Our Connected World," Gizmodo, January 6, 2015, https://paleofuture.gizmodo.com/nikola-teslas-incredible-predictions-for-our-connected-1661107313.

and, yes, malware that modern smartphones deliver to billions of users. Fortunately, there are many antivirus software remedies available, including Avast, Bitdefender, and Norton for Android devices and Avast, Avira, and Lookout for iOS used in iPhones. While smartphones are being increasingly used as primary computing devices by many, they are much easier to manage and keep free of malware than any desktop or laptop PC, so I don't recommend any particular security software solution for most smartphone users due to the more tightly controlled security and monitoring of software installations on mobile devices.

 **SENIOR CYBER TIP:** Malware is malicious software written by cyberthieves for the purpose of theft, solicitation of personal information, or destruction of data. Malware is truly sneaky because it can be introduced to your computer or smartphone undetected and stay in there for years. Some malware steal passwords,

some generate digital currency, and some will spy on you—but all are unwelcome visitors and can do serious damage if left unchecked.

KEEP IT SIMPLE

If you are contemplating getting a smart-phone but aren't sure whether you can operate it—or perhaps your kids got you a smart-phone as a gift, and you are overwhelmed—I would suggest getting one like the Jitter-bug cell phone. You've probably heard about them and for good reason. They are popu-lar among the senior crowd for their compact flip-phone design, easy-to-push buttons, large text displays, and reasonable monthly rates. Plans start at $14.99 per month, giving you peace of mind and the ability to reach out to a loved one at any time for help or just to say hello.

Jitterbug's brand identity is "Simplicity for everyone." Their standard phone plans are just that: *phone plans*. There are no data caps, texts, or apps to install or manage. That simplicity means not only less hassle but also fewer security and privacy problems.

Even the most sophisticated smartphone available today is susceptible to all sorts of malware, and because modern smartphones are always connected to the internet, they can have a host of possible threats hidden within web browsing, email, apps, and text messaging. I'm not dismissing the conveniences and features that smartphones provide, but there is a rule in the cybersecurity world: more convenience goes hand in hand with less security. As companies make things easier on these devices—like online shopping, communications, and software installation—hackers find new ways to exploit all kinds of features.

From a cybersecurity perspective, many hackers have shifted their attention to smartphones due to all of the added conveniences. If you care about taking great pictures, you'll need the latest smartphone with the latest camera sensor and software. If you want to stay in touch with friends and family through Facebook, you'll need to install the app and probably other associated apps (such as Facebook Messenger) on your device. If you want turn-by-turn directions when driving, you will need to keep your global positioning system (GPS) app on and remember to turn it off when you are not traveling to ensure no one can track you. All these convenience choices require security tradeoffs.

I recommend anyone who feels unsure about their smartphone data take technology in bite-size steps. If you're new to mobile phones, start with a basic Jitterbug. If you feel you've moved beyond that type of phone's limitations, you can always upgrade to a Jitterbug "simple smartphone" with a full touchscreen but limited to only certain apps. If you feel confident enough to engage in social media and can't live without those grandchildren pics, it might be time to take off the training wheels and go with a fully functioning smartphone.

CHOICES AND MORE CHOICES

There are basically two *operating systems* spread among many different brands and phone manufacturers, but the choice you make essentially boils down to the people you know. If you want to stay in touch with friends and family who primarily use Apple's iPhone, then it's best to get an iPhone. If they mostly use the Android platform (which includes Samsung, OnePlus, or Google Pixel phones, among many others), go with Android.

There is no wrong choice here, because all the various operating systems and phones work with each other. All phone makers are looking to wow customers with their unique features, but at the end of the day, it's all just bits and bytes that any computer can understand. This means any picture you take on your phone can be viewed on any other smartphone that receives your pic and vice versa. The same goes for apps like Facebook and the text messages you send too.

Blue Versus Green

I don't want to get bogged down in the geek-tails (geeky details) here, but I would be remiss if I didn't mention at least one caveat to my earlier statement about all technology working well together. Since all phone makers are continually looking to stand out from the pack, they all introduce features and services that make their products special. Apple has famously created a platform that stands out for its simplicity and security features. Unfortunately, this has led to the exclusion of some users who do not own Apple products or use their services, specifically Apple Messages, which is Apple's own text messaging service.

SENIOR CYBER TIP: When readable data or content is mathematically converted into a secret code to prevent unauthorized access, that content is **encrypted**. For example, iPhones use a secure text messaging system that keeps all messages private for its users. The users' texts appear as blue bubbles to indicate that they are **encrypted** so no one (not even Apple) can read them unless the user wants to share them. Android users can send and receive messages to any iPhone user, but the non-iPhone messages appear as green bubbles to indicate they do not contain an extra layer of security.

So far so good. However, problems can arise when group texts are created and shared. Android phone users cannot be included in group texts created on an iPhone, so the "green-bubble people" tend to be left out of picture and message sharing. Many users have engineered their own workarounds to receive emails or texts separately from the group, but some find it too difficult to maintain these digital lifestyles and give up by either adopting the dominant platform or just living without those baby pics.

OLD SCHOOL

Many users prefer the desktop experience, and why not? Large screens and physical keyboards are easy on the eyes and joints. The "iPhone elbow" is already being diagnosed by doctors around the world. It can happen to any small touchscreen device user but is essentially the latest source of lateral epicondylitis, tendinitis, and carpel tunnel syndrome. This is due to how users hold and use their devices for hours on end. Desktop and laptop computers, generally, encourage better posture and less joint stress than their mobile counterparts.

These old-school computers also make for great web browsing, emailing, and even gaming. If you want to have a little fun with young kids, simply introduce them to a desktop keyboard and mouse. Most children under age ten were practically born with a touchscreen tablet in their hands and have never used a computer without a touchscreen, so they tend to be baffled by the concept of a computer mouse and physical keyboard.

Seniors might suffer from "senior moments" more than their younger counterparts, but we all suffer from occasional memory lapses and can be confused by new things. The important thing to remember is we are all computing at our own level and have much to learn from each other. Don't hesitate to share your knowledge with others regardless of how tech savvy they may appear. And remember that all technology is just a tool to bring people closer together, not to alienate some and give others a false sense of superiority.

 **SENIOR CYBER TIP:** Do you worry about security and privacy of messages you send to others? If so, pick a phone that supports strong encryption and make sure encryption is always enabled (typically located at the bottom of your phone's SETTINGS menu). Apple tends to have superior encryption capabilities built into its iPhone operating system (OS) platform, but other smartphone makers are also beginning to adopt stronger encryption technology as well.

3

Digital
Communications

Modern digital communications are full of colorful expressions that sound analogous to our physical universe. For example, when you're looking at a website on your computer or smartphone, that is called "surfing." And since we cannot connect internet cables directly into our brains, like plugging in a stereo, we must use a visual interface called a **browser** to see the websites.

SURF'S UP

So we browse and surf websites on browsers to explore the internet. And on the internet, we are all connected, just not literally. In fact, we are connected only through servers, which are a type of supercomputer that simultaneously serves many thousands of users, much like a large star that serves many planets. These servers are typically located in large data centers. Large companies like Netflix, Facebook, or Google are similar to galaxies housing many thousands of servers all networked together, kind of like the millions of stars in each galaxy. When you text, email, or videochat with a friend, your data center is simply connecting to your friend's data center through the internet; it's kind of like a single telephone switchboard operator working a million simultaneous connections.

 **SENIOR CYBER TIP:** A **web browser** like Google Chrome or Safari is a program used to look at web pages located on

the internet, while a **search engine** is a website, like Google, Yahoo, or Bing, that allows you to search for information found on web pages. Search engines and their results are viewed in a web browser.

With all of these billions of connections through many servers happening at the speed of light, a system is needed to organize and locate each and every device, no matter where they are. Fortunately, the millions of servers across the internet can use your IP address to connect.

 **SENIOR CYBER TIP:** An **internet protocol (IP) address** is a unique numerical label assigned to each device connected to a computer network that uses the internet protocol for communication. IPs are kind of like landline phone numbers because they identify you or your household based

on your general location. When your home is connected to the internet, it is assigned an IP number that might look something like **216.6.141.73**. That single IP address feeds every phone, tablet, and computer in your home, and your wireless router sorts out which device gets which message.

Some internet providers require a separate modem (the device that converts computer data for long-distance transmission to other computers) and router hardware for a connection, while others include both functionalities built into a single piece of hardware. In either case, the router acts like a powerful traffic cop, making sure all data is being sent and received properly to every connected device. Some routers can support up to 250 devices simultaneously, which is more typical for businesses. In the case of mobile devices, users are on the go, but these devices are still assigned specific IP addresses by the wireless carriers that provide data to those devices and their users.

It might seem like I'm going into extra detail here, but there's a reason. When your internet service or computer stops working, you might need technical support. But nobody likes contacting tech support without even knowing how to describe the problem. Just like nobody wants to take a broken-down car into an auto repair shop without knowing what's wrong—or at least being able to describe the problem—the same holds true for technical support. And the only people who like it even less are the tech support employees who will need to help fix the problem. Without a few clues or identifiable symptoms, it's very difficult to troubleshoot a computer problem. So while some of my explanations might feel long-winded, I hope they'll help you rely less on others and perhaps be able to fix problems faster when you must rely on others to fix them.

THE WISDOM OF THE CROWD

You might have heard that, right now, we live in a "golden age of technology." Looking back about twenty-five years ago, it's hard to deny it when you consider how much the internet has changed our lives. Computers and micro-chips have been doubling in speed every one to two years while costing about the same for decades now, and they will continue to do so for some time. While that's great, what really changed the world was the introduction of internet web browsers and search engines.

Just imagine traveling back in time only a few decades and trying to explain the future to people in the 1980s. Technology has become smaller, faster, and more personalized, but that wasn't very difficult to predict. However, how do you explain that in the near future, they will have the ability to get instant answers to any questions from anywhere in the world? Sure, you can get the answers to all kinds of trivia and encyclopedic knowledge, but search engines can do so much more than that.

Crowdsourcing

The wisdom of the crowd cannot be over-stated, and it's not just about finding answers to obscure questions. Crowdsourcing is a key component to search engines because when questions are posed to a search engine, it auto-matically taps into the experiences and skills of billions of people. Got a broken toaster? You can find dozens of videos and how-to advice for how to fix the exact model of your broken toaster right on the Web. Want to learn how to crochet, fix a flat tire, or prepare a souf-flé? It's all on the internet and accessible to any search engine.

About fifteen years ago, my wife and I decided to remodel our kitchen with high-end stainless steel appliances, including a Sub-Zero refrigerator, Wolf oven, and Fisher & Paykel dual dishwasher. These are premium brands, so we realized we were paying for the names as much as we were paying for the value they offered. Nevertheless, they have all functioned flawlessly for over fifteen years . . . until just recently. The oven refused to ignite, so I inquired about a service technician visit and was quoted a $300 service fee, not including the parts!

After recovering from the price shock, I turned to the internet, not to find a competing service fee but to dig a little deeper into the problem itself. I entered the make and model number of our oven into Google. From there I was taken to Reddit.com, where I found many other individuals experiencing the same problem with their ovens. One of the Reddit users took me to YouTube, where I watched a short video created by a user that simply explained the problem and offered a few quick solutions, including step-by-step repair instructions and a source for the replacement parts. Two days later, my twenty-nine-dollar replacement starter arrived from Amazon.com, and about an hour after that, I had disassembled, removed, and replaced the faulty starter thanks to those Reddit and YouTube users and the wisdom of the crowd.

 SENIOR CYBER TIP: Reddit.com is an American social news website that aggregates content and discussions; it is an excellent source for troubleshooting many different types of problems. However, Reddit users set their own rules and tools to customize moderation, so be warned that many posts and discussions can be quite disturbing for some.

4

All Search Engines Are Not Alike

Y ou're not reading this book to brush up on your appliance repair skills; you're reading it for cybersecurity tips and know-how, which is exactly what you can get from any search engine. I always try to surround myself with people much smarter than I am—like engineers, inventors, cryptographers, and security experts—but you would be astounded to learn how many of the "technology experts" fail to use search engines to answer the simplest of questions.

Rather than simply "googling"—which is the verb some use when performing a search on Google—how long their laptop will run on battery power, for instance, they spend time visiting the laptop maker's website, searching for their model, navigating to the technical specifications page, and scrolling down until they find the answer. They could've simply typed "MacBook battery life" into their search engine and been presented with immediate results—or clicked on the first link taking them directly to the laptop's technical specifications page. In any case, clicking, typing, and time are always saved when a search engine is employed.

I realize I am at risk of losing business by saying this, but a decent search engine will also answer 75 percent of your basic security questions instantly. When I say "decent" search engine, I am generally referring to Google. Google (owned by Alphabet, Inc.) is the go-to search engine with around an 80 percent worldwide market share. Eight out of every ten crowdsourcers out there use Google Search on a regular basis because it just works. But not all search engines are created equal. Coca-Cola has its secret recipe, and Google has its own proprietary algorithm designed to produce efficient search results.

GOOGLE'S SECRET SAUCE

Google uses a secret mathematical algorithm to scan the entire internet and index every single web page; then it attempts to match every search request to those indexed pages—nearly immediately.

SENIOR CYBER TIP: Algorithms used in software are sets of rules given to an artificial intelligence (AI) program so it can learn on its own. Algorithms power everything from Facebook news feeds to email spam detection. However, before algorithms can be integrated into AI, they must be written by human engineers;

since humans have innate biases, this can lead to many unintended consequences in the software.

Not much is known about the Google algorithm except it keeps learning and getting better all the time. For instance, Google users don't even need to spell search queries correctly because Google's auto-suggest function works better than any word processing software; the search engine can actually predict what you are searching for before you even type the second letter. This brings me to some of the scarier things about Google and most other search engines.

As powerful as internet search technology is—as well as free to everyone—Google is an advertising business through and through. The company wants to change the world for the better, but it can achieve this only by capturing as much personal information about every one of its users as possible, which is a bit scary. This data is organized into marketable chunks that advertisers can target for a price. Critics are quick to say Google is "selling your data to advertisers." While technically not true, I cannot help but feel the end results are the same, because some advertisers probably know more about my consumer preferences than my friends and family do.

For example, internet users are bombarded with barbeque grill ads just seconds after searching for a simple grilling recipe, and on and on. The data centers storing all this information are heavily secured, but that hasn't seemed to slow the growing trend of massive data breaches. In 2018 alone, there were a reported 945 unique data breaches that led to 4.5 billion compromised data records worldwide. Those are huge and scary numbers and, unfortunately, it's very difficult for any of us to avoid being lumped into those statistics if we want to participate in a digital society. But I *can* offer some tips that will help you feel safer, at the very least.

DUCK DUCK GOOGLE

While Google is the dominant player in the search engine business, there are competent alternatives. Microsoft's Bing boasts some five billion searches by users globally, but more important, Microsoft isn't an advertising company. Its revenue is primarily generated through software, cloud service, and Xbox game console sales. Microsoft still allows advertisers access to data collected from Bing searches, but since most of its revenue comes from hardware and software sales, Bing doesn't collect and store user information in the same way Google does.

 **SENIOR CYBER TIP: Cloud** services (aka "the cloud") refers to massive data centers that can store and manage information for millions of users instead of being stored directly on the users' own computers and taking up valuable storage space. The advantage of using a cloud service is you can access your information on any device with an internet connection. Many companies have their own cloud of networked servers. For example, users of Apple products have their information stored on its proprietary iCloud; Google and Amazon Photos also have their own cloud services. Typically, these services offer a certain amount of data storage for free, and the users must pay a nominal amount for additional storage.

If you visit DuckDuckGo.com, another popular alternative search engine, you'll see something interesting—or rather, it's what you won't see. Search results don't dominate the entire right side of the web page like in Google's search results. That's because unlike Google, DuckDuckGo is a *private* search engine that's pledged to block advertising trackers, keep search histories private, and allow users to maintain control of their personal data. On the right side of every Google search results page, text ads that were paid for by an advertiser appear. Sometimes the ads are helpful, and sometimes they're a nuisance, but since DuckDuckGo does not collect personal user data, it cannot offer targeted data to advertisers.

If you search for local florists on DuckDuckGo, you will find all kinds of links—including some advertisements for local florists—but those advertisers cannot track and serve you more ads across the internet like Google advertisers do. And DuckDuckGo is *not* recording all of your searches in order to build a customer profile that includes your shopping, travel, dining, and work habits. DuckDuckGo not only opposes tracking its users, it claims companies like Google do not even need to track user behavior to the extent they do. Users provide all the data advertisers need simply by typing in a few keywords when they search.

We know this to be true because companies like Facebook have admitted to it while responding to questioning from US senators. In a November 19, 2019, letter written to US Senators Coons and Hawley, Facebook laid out the three ways it physically tracks users' locations and behaviors. It went on to detail those three methods and reveal that even when users turn off location services on their mobile devices, for instance, Facebook still knows where they are based on their interactions with other Facebook users and their IP addresses. As I said before, IP addresses are a requirement for all connected devices, so while a hacker can hide his IP address (through spoofing), it cannot be turned off. Therefore, the only way to keep Facebook from tracking you is never download and install the app in the first place. If you have it on your phone or computer and do not want to be tracked, delete it immediately.

 **SENIOR CYBER TIP: Spoofing** is the act of disguising a communication from an unknown source to make it look as if it were from a known, trusted source. Spoofing can apply to emails, phone calls, and websites, or it can be more technical, such as spoofing a computer's IP address or domain name system (DNS) server.[4] A number of different types of scams use spoofing in various ways.

---

4 "What Is Spoofing? Spoofing Defined, Explained, and Explored," Forcepoint, accessed July 2020, https://www.forcepoint.com/cyber-edu/spoofing.

DATA MATTERS

If data collection isn't great for consumers, why do so many tech companies engage in the practice? There are two reasons:

1. It's highly profitable. All that data provides a treasure trove of details about customers, and advertisers will tell you the more they know about a customer, the more they are willing to pay for that information.

2. Vast user data collection simply works; on a technical level, all that data is used to train and feed the complex

algorithms that tech companies rely on. For example, these algorithms allow voice assistants (like Siri and Alexa) to understand queries in nearly every spoken language—even with thick accents. Additional algorithms can then predict user interest in a particular product and recommend it. That functionality comes only from *massive* data collection from people who are, ultimately and unwittingly, training machines that help artificial intelligence systems to learn faster.

Opting Out

What if you don't want to be tracked, recorded, or solicited electronically? Is there a way to avoid such intrusions without missing out on all the fun of technology? Yes. There are a few simple steps you can take to avoid big tech's reach into your life, and it starts by *not* opting in. All tech companies (even the most invasive ones) require users to opt into agreements, updates, and log-ins. Most tech companies also allow users to experience some or all of their services without creating and logging in to their accounts. For instance, Google Search and Google Maps do not require users to log in to function. This means you can get all the search results you want and go anywhere with turn-by-turn directions without having to worry about being tracked, provided you are not logged in while doing so.

Due to excessive strain on batteries, many mobile devices—including iPhone and Android smartphones—will alert users to apps that are being used in the background. The notifications educate users not just about their device's power but also about the many points of data covertly being collected by apps, including locations, user contacts, and microphone and camera data. Users can choose to delete any "offending" apps or modify the app's behavior so data is retrieved only while that app is actively being used. On smartphones, these choices can be made in the Settings function.

Your habits and patterns will still be analyzed and stored with others as a collective by using a technique called differential privacy, which is simply a way to share data about groups of people without revealing anything about specific users in that group. It's a very useful tool for artificial intelligence (AI) purposes but not nearly as useful to advertisers because it can deliver ads only to large groups versus specific customers.

Due to this limitation, companies like Google and Amazon allow the aforementioned services, such as mapping and searching, to be used anonymously but with diminished features while promoting new and amazing services that function only after customers hand over their data. It may seem harmless, but forcing customers to trade their personal privacy for better experiences can add up to an Orwellian nightmare.

In 2020, China's "social credit system" went live for over a billion Chinese citizens. This system uses a vast array of AI facial recognition and data tracking systems to dispense or subtract social credits from an individual's account based on their daily actions. Infractions as mild as jaywalking can purportedly lead to stiff penalties, including personal travel restrictions, until they earn more credits for doing good deeds as defined by the government. China's social credit system for encouraging good behavior from its population is an extreme example of how personal data can be used to control or manipulate. As we continue to rely more on AI devised by big technology corporations, we can expect to see similar examples here in America, too, unless steps are taken to keep overreaching technology at bay.[5]

5 Christina Zhou and Bang Xiao, "China's Social Credit System Is Pegged to Be Fully Operational by 2020—But What Will It Look Like?" Australian Broadcasting Corporation, January 1, 2020, https://www.abc.net.au/news/2020-01-02/china-social-credit-system-operational-by-2020/11764740.

There's nothing unsafe about using a popular service that requires some of your personal data while using it. You can always create an account, log in, get what you need, and log back out. The trick is remembering to log out when you are finished. Otherwise, the company will continue tracking your every move, and they will *never* remind you to log out.

SENIOR CYBER TIP: If you've already opted into a service you enjoy using, be sure you are logged out when not using it. Some apps can continue to collect data about you even if you are not logged in, so be sure to set access limitations under each app's settings.

5

Internet Undertow

Now that you know the pros and cons of web surfing, browsing, and performing searches on the internet, I can warn you about some of the pitfalls. Browsers are powerful software programs, but they can be used only when you're connected to the internet. Once connected, however, a browser conveniently allows users to explore millions of websites by tracking and storing all of your visits and searches by default. This might seem like a privacy violation, but to some extent, we are all giving up our privacy just by downloading and agreeing to use a web browser as designed.

Look at it this way: Some people enjoy shopping, staying at hotels, or dining out in places that recognize them and offer perks like skipping ahead of the wait line or a getting quiet corner table. Others enjoy the anonymity of using cash and not being recognized by anyone, no matter how or where they spend their money. Browsers function more like the former by default, and some websites require quite a bit of personal information from you, especially if you want to avoid the "inconveniences" of digital life.

We've all experienced the internet inconveniences of being required to enter your name or email address and password every time you visit a particular website. Entering the information once is fine, but can you imagine needing to state your name and room number *every* single time you entered your hotel? That would quickly grow tiresome. So browsers automatically recognize you and your preferences when you visit websites with something called "cookies."

 **SENIOR CYBER TIP: Cookies** are simple tracking codes that websites use to remember products you browsed, your log-in credentials, and other things about your digital persona.

Cookies do not know what you are wearing, how much money you have in your savings account, or other more personal things. Cookies do know, on any given web page, which items you clicked on, how long you stayed on that page, and the website you just came from. The important thing to remember about cookies is that they can be turned off or erased in any browser at any time. The only question to ask yourself is: *Can I live without them now that I know how much convenience they afford me?*

BROWSER BASICS

Google's Chrome, Mozilla's Firefox, and Micro-soft's Internet Explorer and Edge are the top three web browsers and account for nearly 90 percent of all PC (Windows-based personal computer versus Apple computer) browser use in the United States,[6] but there are other browsers and means of browsing than just on a PC. For instance, Apple's Safari browser comes preinstalled on all Apple computers, iPad tablets, and iPhones (the most popular

---

6 Gregg Keizer, "Top Web Browsers 2020: Edge Makes Double Digits," Computerworld, November 2, 2020, www.computerworld.com/article/3199425/top-web-browsers-2020-edge-makes-double-digits.html?page=35.

smartphone in the United States). However, if you do not have a smartphone, you are less likely to be using Safari to browse. That means most iPhone users (and Apple/Mac computer households) use only Safari and might not even know about the other popular browsers. The various features and idiosyncrasies among all the browsers are extensive, but I will discuss some of them in terms of their respective platforms' overall approach to security.

All browsers allow cookies to be disabled, website visit history to be cleared, and private browsing modes to be enabled. Some browsers go a little further than others to protect your privacy by default, while others seem to hide those protections in order to gather more data about you.

All new computers include the latest browser software preinstalled, but older machines are reliant on their owners for the latest software. Many legacy computer hardware and websites still require outdated browsers, such as Microsoft's Internet Explorer, which once boasted about 96 percent of all web browsing usage at its peak in 2002[7] but has since dropped to around 8 percent.[8] Microsoft saw this decrease in popularity coming long ago and introduced a more modern browser called Edge to take the place of Internet Explorer before completely dropping support for the aging browser. Unfortunately, there are still millions of users out there running the outdated, unsecure Internet Explorer as their only connection to the internet. This sends shivers down the backs of security experts' spines. Not only are millions of people vulnerable to viruses, malware, and a host of other computer problems as a result of this outdated software, but Microsoft no longer issues security patches or fixes for the older versions. I urge anyone currently using Internet Explorer

---

7 Robert Darrell, "Internet Explorer," Ironspider, accessed July 2020, http://www.ironspider.ca/browsers/ie7.htm.

8 Gregg Keizer, "Top Web Browsers 2020: Edge Makes Double Digits," Computerworld, November 2, 2020, www.computerworld.com/article/3199425/top-web-browsers-2020-edge-makes-double-digits.html?page=35.

to switch over to Edge by downloading it directly from www.microsoft.com/edge.

Apple computers accounted for only about 13 percent of all computers sold in the United States in 2020, but the company has the most robust security for their users.[9] There are multiple reasons for this, but even if you live in the Apple ecosystem, you may not be aware of some of the benefits. I recommend you look past the sticker price of Apple products and consider the extended life span, security benefits, and amenities that make the Apple ecosystem so attractive to its loyal users.

 **SENIOR CYBER TIP:** Because Apple has a minority market share in computers, it is a much smaller target for hackers than the many Windows-based PCs in use. However, since most hacking is

9 Thomas Alsop, "Apple's Market Share of PC Unit Shipments in the United States from 2013 to 2020, by Quarter," Statista, July 24, 2020, https://www.statista.com/statistics/576473/united-states-quarterly-pc-shipment-share-apple/.

conducted through the internet, and all modern computers and smartphones support all browsers, *the browser remains the most crucial security defense* for your computing needs. Choose your browser based on its level of security, not just its features and looks.

6

A Little Education Is a Good Thing

The general rule for all tech products is: *If you're not paying for the product, you are the product.* While this statement might sum up the tech world for some, the real tech world is less polarized. It's important to educate yourself about the key players in tech just like baseball fans educate themselves about the players on and off the field. Not all companies are cut from the same cloth, and no one knows this better than tech journalists. Like a good movie reviewer, good tech journalists won't tell you what to think. Rather, they will explain how *they* think and feel about a company or product; therefore, you can come to your own conclusions by using their opinions as a baseline.

Once you avail yourself of online tech and news publications, such as Yahoo, CNET, and *Wired*—and even more activist organizations like the nonprofit digital rights group Electronic Frontier Foundation (EFF)—you will quickly begin to see which tech companies try to protect the digital rights of their users and which ones continually find themselves in hot water. I'm not asking readers to research and weigh every option before choosing. On the contrary, tech news journalists have already done most of this work for you, so it's important to give more weight to their opinions than those of more traditional news sources like Fox News or CNN.

IN YOUR MAILBOX

The United States Postal Service (USPS) was created in 1792 under the first post-master general, Benjamin Franklin. Due to the physical nature of postal mail and pack-ages, you might be wondering how the USPS ties into cybersecurity, but several hundred years of postal scams have not gone unno-ticed by modern cyberthieves. While I use email and texts as my primary method of communication, I am still bombarded by junk mail delivered to my home every day. In fact, the average American receives forty-one pounds of junk mail per year, according to the Sightline Institute.[10] Much of this is harmless solicitation, but how can one know which ones mean to sell us something and which ones intend to steal our money?

I like to err on the side of caution for all snail mail (old-fashioned postal delivery). I treat every piece of mail I receive as a security threat unless I was expecting to receive mail from that person or company listed on the return address. This includes official-looking letters from the DMV, sweepstakes, coupons, various charities, and even the US government. Modern offset printing is cheap and highly accurate, so there isn't an envelope or letterhead in existence that cannot be copied and manipulated to serve criminal intentions.

Junk mail can be truly challenging to identify at first glance. Recently, my wife received a nondescript white envelope

---

10 Alan Durning, "Junk Mail Box: Stopping Paper Waste; Un-spamming snail mail," Sightline Institute, December 31, 2007, https://www.sightline.org/2007/12/31/junk-mail-box-stopping-paper-waste/.

from MetaBank, a bank she never knew existed. The weight and feel of the envelope suggested some kind of plastic credit card was enclosed. This is a common junk mail promotion tactic from many banks and retailers, so it seemed to confirm her suspicions that it was a piece of junk mail. However, when she opened it up to throw the card into the shredder, she noticed it appeared to be a debit card. She put it to the side for me to take a look at when I got home.

On May 18, 2020, the US Treasury Department announced that approximately four million Americans who have not yet received their stimulus payment via check or direct deposit would instead receive a debit card. Those final debit cards were the balance of the $2 trillion COVID-19 stimulus package approved by Congress known as the CARES Act. Fortunately, we discovered this little-known piece of news just before our debit card was headed for the shredder. The poor communication on the part of the US government is just one of many examples why we must spend a modicum of our time vetting the legitimacy of our physical mail.

There are a few things you can do to minimize the amount of junk mail you receive daily. First, you can register with www. DMAChoice.org, a nonprofit organization that will limit your junk mail for up to ten years by working closely with advertisers to let them know your preferences. In addition, you can register with www.directmail.com for the National Do Not Mail List to limit the amount of junk mail you receive. They, too, have relationships with direct marketing and advertising companies, none of which want to waste money on postage if you plan on throwing out all their mailers. If you want to minimize the number of credit card and insurance policies companies are sending you, try www.OptOutPrescreen.com. This official consumer credit reporting industry website accepts and processes requests from consumers to opt in to or out of these various offers.

The good news is that, unlike email scams (much more on that later), you are free to open any letter addressed to you and inspect it for authenticity. The last thing you want to do is hastily throw out a letter that might contain an unexpected check or correspondence from an old friend. If the letter looks legitimate, the next step is to verify its veracity by calling the number or visiting the website listed. Regardless of which you choose, *never* reveal any private information on a web form or to the person on the other end of the phone or web-chat session. This includes your Social Security number, any account numbers, passwords, or identifying answers to security questions. If any of these organizations are legitimate, they already have some private information about you, so the burden of proof is on *them*, not you.

Scam Alert

All consumer scams start with the scammer casting the widest net. Since 99 percent of targeted consumers do not even respond to the scams, the remaining 1 percent become valuable targets. That is why you should never reply to unsolicited emails, answer robocalls, or supply any personal information to websites you do not already frequent. As soon as you engage with any of these things, your name, number, email, etc., goes on a new list. This new list is like the leads for a desperate salesman trying to sell you something you don't need, except this "salesman" is a crook, probably living in another country, and intent on stealing your money or personal data to sell to another crook.

Of course, there are plenty of legitimate companies out there also looking to gather your personal data. They might not be trying to rob you, but if they are holding on to your data with the intent of selling it to advertisers or other companies, the end results are much the same. Sooner or later, hackers and unscrupulous businesspeople are going to obtain your credentials, so it's always best to withhold your private data from anyone requesting it.

DID YOU KNOW?

Did you know you are not required to provide your Social Security number even to a doctor's office that is treating you? Some offices claim to need your Social Security number just to schedule an appointment or when you sign in at the waiting area.

SENIOR CYBER

Healthcare professionals are free to ask for all kinds of personal information, but you are *never* legally required to provide your Social Security number for anything other than employment, taxes, and banking issues.

I know this because I was once told I had to put my Social Security number on a sign-in sheet at the doctor's office in order to receive care. I saw a list of Social Security numbers already on that sheet from other patients and realized that anyone could simply snap a quick picture of those names and numbers and walk away with enough information to perform dozens of identity thefts. I refused to list something as private as my Social Security number and instead suggested my insurance policy number, name, and birthdate.

They refused, so I asked to speak with someone in charge. The head office administrator could see that I was willing to walk away over this disagreement and quickly

70

accepted my terms. Many healthcare facilities continue to enforce old policies that do not benefit anyone but criminals, and until they are questioned or challenged, they will not even think about changing those outdated policies. Your job as a Senior Cyber is to stay on guard and challenge any systems that can make your life or the lives of those around you unsafe.

Millions of scam letters travel through the US Postal Service every day. One of the more effective scams is the "fake check," which looks legitimate enough to fool a bank temporarily, but that just means you are left holding the bag.

Suppose you receive a check in the mail for $4,120. It looks real enough, so you read the enclosed letter stating you have won an international lottery drawing and the check is your prize. You might not remember even entering any lottery drawing, but you don't want to just throw away the possibility of receiving free money, so you read on. The letter includes specific instructions for you to deposit the check into your account but to also wire a small amount back to the sweepstakes association to cover international taxes and fees. If you are reading this and still don't know whether or not it could be a scam, let me save you the time. It's a scam.

Thousands of scams like these fool Americans every year to the average tune of $2,400 per victim.[11] Some of them come in the form of believable-looking emails, and some include phone numbers for someone to talk you through "the details," but most require a small wire transfer back to the scammers. They do this so they can get your cash quickly while your bank takes a few days to verify whether or not their fake check is worth the paper it is printed upon. Even if you are completely innocent, your bank will discover the fraud and you will still be

---

11 Sandra Latouff, "Meet the Top Ten Scams — #1 fake check fraud," National Consumers League, March 2013, https://www.nclnet.org/ meet_the_top_ten_scams_1_fake_check_fraud.

responsible for paying for any losses or fees incurred. Regardless of how much money we are talking about or how much they seem to know about you, if anyone gives you a check and asks you to send them some money in return, they are a scammer. Most scammers we encounter have a detailed story designed to play upon our greed or trust, but remember that the more detailed the story is, generally, the faker it is. But not all scammers interact directly with their victims.

DUMPSTER DIVING

One day I received a new credit card sent to my business from my bank. I followed the instructions to activate my new card and placed it into my wallet. Many card users would be content in just discarding their old card into the trash, but I've seen enough credit fraud to know better, so I cut mine up into tiny pieces with a pair of scissors. After cutting it up into about a dozen small bits of plastic and sprinkling them through-out the garbage can in my office, I thought I had created the impossible-to-solve jigsaw puzzle, but I was in for a surprise.

A few days later, it was garbage collection day on our block, and the day after that, I received a call from my building's mainte-nance supervisor urging me to come outside and see something for myself. I met him by the regular trash pickup area and saw all the fragments of my old, cut-up credit card meticulously pieced backed together on the sidewalk. The card wasn't taped or glued together, so it could not have been used in a card swiper to make any fraudulent purchases, but the name, account number, expiration date, and three-digit code on the back were all legible and could easily be used to make online purchases or sold to cyberthieves for identity theft and more. A warning, perhaps?

Fortunately, I'd received my new card because my old card was days away from expiration, and by activating my new card, my old card immediately became unusable. However, official mail originating from banks and employers is stolen all the time and used for a variety of monetary purposes and identity theft. I never did discover the person or the motive behind that mysterious card reconstruction, but it certainly required someone willing to get their hands a little dirty, which always puts me on high alert.

 **SENIOR CYBER TIP: Dumpster diving** refers to salvaging the waste in garbage receptacles or dumpsters to find items discarded by their owners, which the picker (or hacker, in some

cases) thinks can be useful in any number of ways.

One Man's Treasure

Dumpster diving is actually a popular pastime among private investigators, hackers, and thieves. Since most garbage receptacles are deemed legal for search by anyone once they are taken off the premises and out to the curb, there is little risk and much more reward than one might think to search through a stranger's refuse.

Your garbage can have true value to a hacker or *anyone* trying to put together the puzzle pieces to form a more complete picture of you. Besides the possibility of finding names, numbers, and even passwords scribbled on notepaper, recent bank statements or deposit slips can provide account origin dates or even your last transaction information. Some banks ask for this information over the phone as security challenge questions to prove your identity. If a hacker successfully answers the questions, they will "become" you for a moment and may be able to gather even more data about you so, next time, they can become you for a little longer, until they are finally able to change your passwords or lock you out of your account just long enough to deplete all your savings.

To prevent a cybercriminal from using your garbage against you, I recommend using a good paper shredder when disposing of all personal documents. If you go shopping at an office supply store, you will find an array of shredders. Most of these shredders fit into one of three categories with prices ranging from $25 to $300, depending on size and level of desired security. The three basic levels of shredder are strip-cut (cuts forty to fifty strips), crosscut (cuts two hundred small squares) and micro-cut (cuts two thousand tiny pieces of confetti).

The micro-cut shredder does a great job shredding paper documents and even expired credit cards, which goes a long way to assuage someone like me who's had their cut-up credit card reconstructed for them as some sort of prank or threat. Rest assured: micro-cut shredders obliterate all readable documents into more pieces than a ticker tape parade.

 SENIOR CYBER TIP: Before throwing out any correspondence, life insurance documents, bills, or even plastic credit or debit cards, shred them beyond recognition with a quality shredder.

7

Electronic Mail, aka Email

N ow that we've covered some of the security pitfalls with old-fashioned snail mail, it's time to move back into the twenty-first century. Email has technically been around for more than fifty years, but it hasn't changed much in the past sixteen years since Google first introduced Gmail. The second most popular email service in the world with a market share of 26 percent, Gmail use is just under Apple's iPhone native mail app with 28 percent.[12] But since you can access your Gmail account on an iPhone, Android, or just about any other device in existence, Gmail addresses are the most common. If you receive a message from anyone with an address ending in @gmail.com, they are a Gmail user.

In 2004, Google gave away millions of Gmail accounts, including a full gigabyte (GB) of space to anyone who signed up. At that time, two to four megabytes (MB) was the standard storage giveaway for most email services. One GB is equal to one thousand MBs, so Google was offering users almost one thousand times more storage space for free. This led to instant adoption of Gmail by millions of users, but it also led to massive amounts of data collection and advertising to those same users by Google.

We've already covered some of the problems involving mass digital data collection, so I won't

---

12 Zia Muhammad, "What's the Most Widely Used Email Client in the World?" Digital Information World, April 10, 2019, https://www.digitalinformation-world.com/2019/04/most-popular-email-clients-worldwide.html.

belabor those points. However, there are still many security risks just from using an email service that knows little to nothing about you. All email services are based on the same fifty-year-old technology that didn't use any kind of anti-spam, security, or encryption technology. While many security measures are now being taken, it's good to know about potential email issues with your data.

 **SENIOR CYBER TIP: Encryption** is the process of encoding a message so only authorized parties with the key can read that message. Encryption protects users from their private data being used against them and can even protect companies from being forced to reveal that private data.

Email addresses have become the default identity of internet users, and like the old white pages in the phone book, most email address are public and easy to find. This makes communication convenient but security a nightmare. Just imagine if we were all identified by our phone numbers, the same phone numbers listed publicly, instead of our names or Social Security numbers. Those same phone numbers could also be anonymously created by anyone, allowing most people to have multiple numbers, which is akin to having multiple identities. You can see why criminals love both the anonymity and the vulnerability of email. Since we all use email as a personal identifier for log-ins, accounts, and correspondences, the number of attacks involving email continues to grow.

PHISH IN A BARREL

In cybersecurity, phishing is spelled differently than the kind involving poles, bait, and a hook, but the scammer's objective is always the same: catch the unsuspecting victim (the phish) in any way you can.

SENIOR CYBER TIP: Phishing is the name for a scam in which a person is duped (through deceptive email, phone call, text message, or letter) into revealing personal or confidential information the scammer can use illicitly.

Remember when the Democratic National Committee (DNC) was hacked in 2016? That all started when a phishing email was sent to Hillary Clinton's campaign chairman, John Podesta, that warned: "Someone just used your password to try to sign in to your Google Account," and continued with: "Google stopped this sign-in attempt. You should change your password immediately."[13] A link followed immediately after the message. Unfortunately, Mr. Podesta reacted out of fear or impatience and didn't think about his actions before taking

13 Tara Golshan, "How John Podesta's Email Got Hacked, and How to Not Let It Happen to You," *Vox*, October 28, 2016, https://www.vox.com/policy-and-politics/2016/10/28/13456368/how-john-podesta-email-got-hacked.

them. Rather than typing the Gmail.com Uniform Resource Locator (URL) address directly into his browser or clicking on his browser's saved Gmail bookmark to check the veracity of this unexpected message, he probably wanted to save a few seconds by clicking directly on the link the criminals included in their email to him.

However, by clicking on that link created by the hackers, Podesta unknowingly handed over his password to them. It didn't matter how long or complex his password was, because he literally spelled it out for the hackers when he thought he was logging into the real Gmail server. From that point on, the criminals were able to simply log in as if they were Podesta to read his confidential emails, copy them, and use them against him and the campaign.

 **SENIOR CYBER TIP:** A **URL** is the acronym for the Uniform Resource Locator that typically begins with "https://www." This is similar to your home's mailing address in that all websites have a destination

URL. URLs can be typed directly into the text field at the top of every browser.

Cybercriminals target their victims through email by first creating a sense of urgency. The subject and body of the message contain alarming words, such as *alert, warning, act now,* and *hurry.* Like a limited-time sale, phishers want their phish to react quickly and take the bait without thinking. This is, in fact, emotional manipulation furthered by emails that resemble real emails from the real companies. Phishing email messages from Apple, Amazon, Microsoft, eBay, and Facebook have all been meticulously recreated so the logos, fonts, wording, and email designs all match the current look from each company. No company is safe from being spoofed (meaning illegally copied) in this way. I have included many visual examples of email phishing scams in the appendix section ("Senior Scams and What to Look For") of this book at the end. After you finish reading this chapter, feel free to jump to the appendix to see whether you can spot the telltale signs of phishing attacks.

Modern operating systems will notify and warn you about *all* software download attempts. Depending on the specific operating system (OS), sometimes multiple warning pop-up windows will appear, asking, "Are you sure you want to download this file from an unknown source?" Other operating systems simply notify users the file has been downloaded and can be found in the Downloads folder. Because of these warnings, most users never get far enough to download and actually launch malware on their own computers, so the vast majority of phishing attacks are simply weblinks that claim to take users to a known website but actually take them elsewhere. Once there, users will see familiar-looking graphics and text requesting log-in credentials, but don't be fooled. Once you submit your email and password to a hacker, they can log in to your email or bank account for years without you knowing about it. If you ever suspect you may have been fooled into revealing your log-in credentials, change them immediately. It takes only a minute to do so, and you could be saving yourself years of trouble.

If you are contacted by any company or individual urging you to change your credentials for security reasons, never click on any links included in their message. Even if the email is legitimate, it's good practice and only takes a second to type in the proper URL and navigate to your account settings from there. And if you accidentally click on an unknown link before you think, don't worry. So long as you haven't provided any secure login information or installed any software onto your computer, you are still safe and secure. Simply stop where you are, close and quit all browser windows and applications, and delete that suspicious email before you resume your work.

Scammers can often go even further by including your personal information, such as name, account number, or phone number, which they easily scraped (extracted data from websites) off the internet, bought from a massive data breach, or even obtained through some dumpster diving. This type of information allows them to send seemingly credible-looking emails directly to the users with their full names. The message sounds urgent and usually involves an account or password that might have been compromised. Clickable links to the account are conveniently included within the email. Every fiber of your being is telling you to log in, investigate, and put a stop to this breach of your account.

But what *should* you do?

STOP. THINK. VERIFY.

Phishing Tricks

Stop whatever you are doing and inspect the email, and in particular, look at the email address of the sender, which is often long and not linked to the company it purports to represent at all. Remember that you are in no immediate danger regardless of what the unexpected message wants you to think. Even if the message is legitimate and there is a real data breach or issue with your account, there is absolutely *no* risk in taking a moment to remove yourself from the emotion of an email to analyze the content and determine the actual sender.

Does the wording read as you would expect from this sender? The majority of phishing emails are created by clever hackers, but English is often not their primary language. Look for any telltale misspellings, improperly used apostrophes, erroneous plurals, and uncommon grammatical choices, as they will reveal themselves if you take the time to read the entire email message a few times.

Now that you've perused the attention-grabbing email, forget the message itself and ask yourself: *Why me?* and *Why now?* Was a massive data breach in the news recently? Remember that even if you are part of that breach, scammers also read the news and have used many scary headlines to terrify users into revealing much more private data than was initially leaked in the actual breach. Was this email created just for you, or could many others be receiving the same message? Remember the wisdom of the crowd? Search for the subject line and a few other pertinent details, using your favorite search engine. Do you see others expressing the same concerns over similar emails, or do you see them explaining why this email is a phishing scam? I've overwhelmingly found the latter to be the case when I've put questions like this into Google Search.

You can also save yourself some time by simply looking at the domain the email originated from or the domain within any links in the email. A domain is a little like a street address. If even one character is off, it will not reach its final destination. Scammers count on people overlooking these types of things, so they sometimes create domains that look similar to the real ones, knowing the recipients might look at support@anazon.com and think they see support@amazon.com. They look similar but are two entirely different domains.

If, after all of your introspection and sleuthing, you still cannot be sure what to believe, there is a very fast and simple remedy: Go directly to the website that sent you the email, log in to it, and see for yourself *or* call their official phone number from their real website and talk to an actual employee from the company. *Never* use the links or phone numbers provided in any email. There is no need to because if you are logging in to your account, you would have to enter your username and password on their website anyway to access your account. The hackers are counting on their victims simply clicking on the "Amazon link" they provided in the email, as opposed to simply typing amazon.com into their browser and then logging into their account. Once logged into your real account, if there is a problem or security prompt, you will see it immediately. The link provided in the email saves you absolutely no time, and everyone knows this, including the real companies—which is why you will never see any direct links in security-related emails from real companies. They know their regular visitors get to them through browser bookmarks, ads, or search engine links.

And if you feel more comfortable speaking to a support or account representative from the company, phone numbers are readily displayed on every company's contact web page and even directly within many search engine results. Some phishing operations are quite elaborate and feature fake phone operators trying to elicit personal information from victims while their fake web pages also try to capture log-in credentials from those who do not wish to use the phone. You might have to wait patiently through a phone navigation menu, but at least you know you'll be speaking with a real company employee and not a crook.

Concerned consumers should report all suspicious email messages to antifraud organizations, such as www.ftc.gov/complaint and reportphishing@antiphishing.org by forwarding the entire email to them.

 **SENIOR CYBER TIP:** If you receive an email you were not expecting, *never* click on any link or attachment unless you are 100 percent sure the communication is real and you trust the sender.

8

Password Protection

My brother, Craig, who's also the coauthor of this book, has a father-in-law who has become infamous around his house for writing every password and squirreling away the scraps of paper in a plastic bag. Every time he helps his father-in-law activate a new device or reset a password, the entire household enters into an almost solemn atmosphere because they know the next fifteen minutes will be devoted to the regular tradition of rifling through the bag of old and new passwords in order to find the one they need.

I suppose he should, at least, set up his father-in-law with some kind of Rolodex or notebook for all those passwords, but Craig doesn't want to encourage unsafe security behavior. After all, cybersecurity experts agree that scribbling passwords on anything will generally lead to those passwords being stolen and used by someone. Also, his father-in-law is in his midseventies, and, let's face it, he probably won't want to change the system he has in place. I suspect he's not the only one storing and retrieving passwords in this manner.

I must confess, I used to subscribe to a similar method of password management, but I employed a thick black binder full of usernames, emails, and passwords, each laser printed on its own slip of paper. It was kind of like a scrapbook, except it contained hundreds of valuable company accounts instead of fond memories. I kept this binder locked in my desk, which was located in my locked office inside my locked corporate headquarters.

It seemed secure enough at the time, but it didn't travel with me, so logging into various accounts became an inconvenience whenever I was away from my desk. I caught myself jotting down a few passwords here and there to continue my work uninterrupted. Of course, I'm a cybersecurity expert whose work is to help others (and myself) stay safe, so I could see I was heading into a conundrum. I decided to look into a few options.

PASSWORD MANAGERS

Password management has become a hot sector in the cybersecurity industry. Although it doesn't sound sexy or high tech, password manager apps do check all the boxes for consumers looking to make life a little easier and a lot safer. The most popular password management services work in the cloud, have both free and paid versions, and can remember the most complex passwords for you. Of course, you must remember a single master password to unlock all those passwords, but once you commit one strong password to memory, you're ready for the internet fast lane.

 **SENIOR CYBER TIP:** Dashlane, LastPass, and 1Password are the three biggest players in the password management space. I've been using Dashlane for the past few years, so I can recommend it to anyone looking to bump up their convenience without sacrificing security.

Do a quick password count in your head. Do you have five passwords? Ten passwords? I'll bet if you keep thinking about it, you'll come up with even more passwords. Many people have more than one hundred. And don't forget about family members and all their accounts. It adds up, which is why password managers also offer family plans. Free trial offers give users a great feel for a service's value to them. If you join Dashlane's free plan, you can manage up to fifty passwords on a single device. If you decide you like it or quickly outgrow the free plan, the upgraded service is only five dollars a month. If learning a new password management program sounds too daunting or you just don't know where to start, try Googling keywords, such as "how to use a password manager" and maybe the name of a particular password manager you have chosen just to get down to the nitty-gritty faster. Choose a video or web page to view directly, and voilà: your first tutorial on password management.

If managing hundreds of passwords across several devices sounds like too much, I have a simpler and more fun way to keep track of passwords: passwordsFAST is a compact, electronic password keeper that anyone can manage. It looks like a calculator but has a tiny QWERTY (top row of letters on your keyboard starting from the left) standard keyboard layout. It fits into any pocket or purse, so you can whip it out and access up to 125 long and complex passwords. Of course, you will still have to enter passwords manually, but having access to all of your passwords in one physical device feels nice.

You don't need an internet connection to use it, and best of all, passwordsFAST costs only $24.99.

Maybe the idea of typing in all of your passwords manually each time doesn't appeal to you. I don't blame you, which is why most browsers and computer operating systems have got you covered. The first time you log in to a website or smartphone app, you should be prompted with a dialogue box that asks whether you want the browser or operating system to remember the password you just entered. Don't worry—if you are already on a trusted site or app, the message is real and trying to be helpful. Once you agree to this, your log-in credentials will automatically be filled in for you each time you log in to that particular website or app. This will even work across all of your devices automatically, providing you are using a cloud service, such as Apple's iCloud, Microsoft's OneDrive, or Google Drive, and use the same master password to unlock all of your devices.

Similarly, search browsers can also provide basic password management for all types of websites and services across the internet, but this is where things get a little stickier. For years, cybersecurity experts have been criticizing tech companies and their users for letting their browsers manage so many passwords, and the criticism is legitimate. The most popular browsers, including Chrome, Firefox, and Safari, have all revealed saved user passwords for any computer novice taking a few simple steps. So while I cannot, in good conscience, recommend any browsers to manage your passwords safely, I can still try to educate readers on all the options available.

THE SECURITY TRIANGLE

There are no silver bullets or bulletproof security solutions, and there are no hard-and-fast rules, either, but this simple security concept can inform every decision made by companies, their customers, and even security experts. And it's not just for security or data-centric products—all electronic products are vulnerable to some kind of security threat, so the security triangle applies to all of them.

The triangle's three points are functionality, security, and usability. The closer you move toward any one of those attributes, the further away you get from the other two. Many security systems, particularly the ones built for consumers, adjust all three of those qualities so that no one will overpower the other two, which leads to a relatively safe, easy-to-use, and useful experience for average consumers.

By contrast, a security system designed for a secret national agency, for example, would offer much greater security than usability or functionality. That is understandable, since most agencies of this kind are protecting national secrets and many lives. The problem occurs when security technology intersects with the real world, one populated by human beings full of emotions, gullibility, and poor judgment. So while the most secure approach might assume the security corner of the triangle is the best place to live, humans are not built that way. If the only way users are going to manage their passwords is through a less-secure web browser, then maybe that is the best way for them.

 SENIOR CYBER TIP: Now that you know the core components of any electronic product are functionality, security, and usability, make sure you use products with a good balance of all three components. But if you are especially worried about your data, choose products that reside closer to the security area within the security triangle.

9

No Two Fingerprints Are the Same

Fortunately, some of the smartest companies and experts are working on ways to encourage users to adopt more security. Over the past few years, biometric security has made incredible gains. The days of covert, underground military bases as the only places that require retina and fingerprint scans are a thing of the past. These days, every modern smartphone contains some form of biometric scanning technology. Samsung Galaxy phones scan their users' retinas to verify their identities. The newest Huawei smartphones not only scan your fingerprints instantly but do so from under the main display. And Apple's iPhone can scan your entire face in virtually any lighting condition to authenticate the user. These high-tech biometric security features are fun and easy to use, but something else is going on here.

 **SENIOR CYBER TIP: Biometric security** is the verification of identity through unique physical characteristics, such as fingerprints, voice, facial features, and retinal attributes. You might not need a password to log in, but if your account is compromised, the data is safe because your personal attributes cannot be replicated by anyone else.

When Apple offered users a choice to bypass the standard four- or six-digit personal identification number (PIN) security code and introduced its proprietary fingerprint scanner

(Touch ID) in 2013, it made huge waves in the smartphone and security industries. Not only did the experts deem fingerprints more secure than entering four-digit PINs, according to studies, Touch ID was responsible for an increase in consumers' security awareness and implementation. When surveyed about their security habits, people preferred fingerprint scanners in their phones to entering a PIN code manually or no code at all. It's the people who adopted fingerprint scanning over using no code at all who got security researchers really excited. By *not* implementing a PIN or passcode to lock their devices, these consumer holdouts were vulnerable to innumerable hackers and thieves; however, when the right technology was introduced at the right time, all parties (except thieves and hackers) truly benefited. My own mother refused to use any PIN to unlock her iPhone for years, but the advent of fast and secure biometric scanning has finally moved her into the twenty-first century.

IT TAKES TWO (FACTORS)

At some point, you might have seen security prompts urging you to enable two-factor or multifactor authentication for your various accounts, especially those involving money. These reminders can be annoying, but they are important and demonstrate good security intentions from the companies. I've always preached that security is achieved in layers, and two-factor authentication is one of the best examples.

 **SENIOR CYBER TIP: Two-factor authentication (2FA)** is also known as multifactor authentication. It is an extra layer of security that requires

not only a password but also another independent factor that can be something a user knows, has in their possession, or is physically unique to that user.

Let's take a moment to go over these different factors of authentication:

1. If an additional factor required is something a user knows, that might be the answer to a security challenge question or an additional password or PIN.
2. If the additional factor is something the user has in their possession, we might be talking about a small security fob that generates passcodes or their smartphone receiving a one-time code via text message.
3. If the security factor requires authentication based on unique physical characteristics of a user, meaning biometrics, that would require the

user's fingerprint, retina, or face to be scanned, for example.

None of these factors are particularly strong by themselves. If someone stole your phone, they would have access to a number of authentication factors, but that's not enough to steal any information from an account protected by 2FA. A typical 2FA account requires a username or email and your password. After entering those credentials, you would then be required to offer an additional factor of proof to access that account. Those extra layers of protection are the backbone of any effective security approach, so if you are prompted to switch to two-factor authentication, I highly recommend it.

THE PASSWORD IS . . .

One of the most effective ways to explain the importance of strong password creation to both a technical and nontechnical person is to show them the numbers. For example, the latest passcode-protected smartphone can be unlocked by your average hacker, depending upon the number of digits you chose to secure your device:

- A four-digit PIN takes about six minutes to crack.
- A six-digit PIN takes a little over ten hours to crack.
- An eight-digit PIN takes a little over a month to crack.
- A ten-digit PIN takes a little over ten years to crack.

There are many factors at play here, but you can quickly see how adding more digits to your passcode can greatly increase the security. And if you add a special character, such as a $ or &, the time it takes a computer to crack the code goes from a decade to hundreds of years. This is because there are a lot special characters on your keyboard, so as soon as you open the possibility of adding special characters or lowercase *and* capital letters together, hundreds of billions more combinations are created for the hacker to try. If you are a password geek like me, go to www.HowSecureIsMyPassword.net and try it out. You can try as many combinations of characters as you like and watch the time it takes to crack go up or down in real time. It's a fun way to stay informed and secure.

Brute Force

Now that you know what a strong password requires, I can share some of the not-so-good password practices I've seen over the years:

1. Never use real words in your passwords. Why? Because real words are listed in the dictionary, and any standard computer

can blaze through the entire English dictionary in less than a second. An effective dictionary attack is automated through software that uses millions of guesses per second in attempt to crack a password.

2. It's also a bad idea to use any pet names, nicknames, birthdates, or addresses in your passwords. Why? Social media sharing and search engines have opened up these once-private names and dates to everyone in the world. I don't want to hurt your ego, but there are thousands more bots and hackers looking at your social media profile page on any given day than your friends and family. Similar to search engine indexing, bots and scripts (automated software programs) are created by hackers to scrape public web pages for personal information automatically. Websites like Facebook, Instagram, and Twitter offer the most personal details about people. These

details are scraped and later sold to other hackers. Sometimes it only takes a matter of hours, and sometimes it might take years, but eventually, enough of these snippets of personal information can be pieced together to hack into users' accounts.

Most TV and movies portray hackers as evil geniuses with an uncanny ability to guess or decipher their victim's password. In actuality, most hackers simply purchase software that can quickly guess passwords, which frees up the hackers to do other things. Any scenario involving multiple guesses until the correct password is guessed is called a brute-force attack, and if you think you've never heard of a brute-force attack, you're probably mistaken.

 **SENIOR CYBER TIP:** A **dictionary attack** is a brute-force technique for defeating an authentication mechanism

by trying millions of likely words in a dictionary that could be part of a password.

In 2014, hundreds of private pictures and data owned by celebrities, including Jennifer Lawrence, Kate Upton, and Kaley Cuoco, were leaked on the internet. You may recall the more sensational headlines claiming that "Apple's iCloud Hacked Revealing Nude Celebrity Photos." The second part of that headline was true, but the iCloud service itself was never hacked; the individual celebrities' accounts were hacked, though, by brute-force attacks.

Each celebrity had shared some private data publicly through their social media or even press interviews. That data was then used in concert with brute-force software to crack each celebrity iCloud account. Since the hackers knew all about their victims, it was a targeted attack, but no computers were illegally accessed, trash cans emptied, or phishing emails deployed. The nature of the celebrities and the poor security they employed on their own accounts helped deliver private password data directly to the hackers.

REUSING PASSWORDS

Some truly unique passwords can be challenging to create and remember, so it's only natural to stick with a good one once you have it. The problem is that once one hacker has it, they have it all. Like a skeleton or master key, reusing passwords will grant thieves access to every single room in your house—even if you've locked all the doors. Never reuse the same password across any websites or account log-ins. Two out of every three internet users reuse passwords, and it shows.

Some security experts, such as Facebook's former chief security officer (CSO) Alex Stamos, believe password reuse is the top cause of harm on the internet.[14] Next time you're in a hurry to

---

14 Katie Collins, "Facebook Buys Black Market Passwords to Keep Your Account Safe," CNET, November 9, 2016, https://www.cnet.com/news/facebook-chief-security-officer-alex-stamos-web-summit-lisbon-hackers/.

create a new account and don't feel like creating a new password, take a moment to create a truly unique password and store it somewhere safe. Those thirty extra seconds can mean the difference between true digital security and a hacking nightmare.

SECURING SOCIAL MEDIA

If you can't resist viewing the latest cat video or posting baby pics on social media, you can, at least, take the necessary precautions so none of your accounts or data are compromised. Don't accept the default settings in any social media account. Remember, social networks make the most revenue by gleaning details about you and then selling ads to companies that care only about selling you merchandise based on those details. Of course, this is usually accomplished through target advertising placed strategically in your news feed or profile page. You will sacrifice no functionality if you turn off many of those data trackers in the settings, especially if you just want to catch up occasionally with some friends and family on the internet.

Most social networks ask for your birthdate when you first sign up. It might seem fun to get automated birthday wishes from your favorite social network and your friends, too, but make no mistake. Facebook cares about your age only so their advertisers can decide whether they should try to sell you sunglasses or bifocals. Your close friends already know your real birthday, so I like to create a new birthday for myself when I sign up for a new social network. It's a fun way to reinvent myself, and more importantly, create a fake birthdate to mess with social networks, their advertisers, and would-be hackers. Of course, you can always opt not to display your real birthdate publicly to anyone in the settings. However, your social network and their advertisers will still have access to that data, so be prepared for some targeted ads.

10

Spam, Spam, Spam

You may not be able to tell your friends exactly when the first spam message was sent, but you can tell them the term originated from an early Monty Python sketch involving some Vikings repeatedly singing the word in a cafe to drown out all other conversation. When your friends ask what that has to do with receiving unsolicited email messages, you can then inform them that the word "spam" was used in message boards in the early 1990s to describe obnoxious and unwanted ads and messages. There is some discrepancy beyond that as to the specific culprits behind spam, but taking early internet users and their sense of humor into account, it's no surprise a Monty Python sketch was involved.

 SENIOR CYBER TIP: Spam is currently used to refer to undesired or unsolicited electronic mail or unwanted messages of any kind. However, **Spam** is also a brand of canned cooked pork made by Hormel Foods Corporation. It was introduced by Hormel in 1937 and gained worldwide popularity after its use during World War II.

I've yet to meet a single internet user who has not received copious amounts of unwanted emails, robocalls, text messages, or other forms of spam advertising. Email messages are, by far, the most common form of spam due to their ubiquity, low cost, and effectiveness. Since email is so common, we all rely on it to keep in touch with others, review online purchase receipts, or conduct business, but spam is effective because it works. Emails can be sent out by the millions from servers anywhere in the world for little more than the cost of electricity to maintain the servers. If only .01 percent of targeted people respond to a spam message, it has done its job. We've all received physical junk mail, so we know to shred it and throw it into the trash. What makes spam any different?

SPAM COUNTERMEASURES

Most spam email is rather harmless, even though it is annoying. Bots scrape the internet daily on web pages, directories, and other email lists for the lowest-hanging fruit of publicly posted emails. Such emails are prime targets for spammers and even some hackers because they are so easily obtained. To combat this, many savvy users create email addresses that function simply as spam countermeasures. These emails may or may not be publicly found, but if they are targeted by spammers, the damage is minimal since they are not connected to any important accounts or log-ins. You can easily create one of these right now for yourself by choosing among a multitude of free email service providers. Simply create a unique email address and a strong password (use at least ten characters) and you can safely enter that email into almost any website. Just make sure you never use the address for something you truly care about—and expect to receive lot of spam.

Unfortunately, many spam messages go beyond harmless solicitation. All spam recipients' actions are trackable. In other words, if you click on any item within a spam email, spammers know you are interested—or at least curious—and your email address goes on a new list of prospective customers or targets. If you make that customer list, you can expect to receive messages to that email address for the rest of its existence. That might sound like bad news, but it's preferable to the alternative, which might include further scams, fraud, and malware.

Needless to say, *never* reply to or click on anything in an email you were not expecting. Even if the email appears to come from a trusted source, if you were not expecting it, then most likely it's a phishing email as previously discussed.

Whether you've already intentionally clicked on some too-good-to-be-true emails or on others by accident, all hope is not necessarily lost. *Legitimate* e-commerce retailers always include an unsubscribe link on the bottom of every email they send. It is also accompanied by the sender's official privacy policy and a link to the company's physical address and contact information. If you remember subscribing to their email list, you can safely click on that bottom link to unsubscribe at any time. Most retailers will honor your request to unsubscribe, but you must make sure you unsubscribe to *all* of their mailing lists. Many retailers have multiple mailing lists that must be individually checked, depending on the language of their unsubscribe web page, so read it carefully.

If you find yourself subscribed to a mailing list that you do not remember opting into, you can still try to unsubscribe by using the unsubscribe link at the bottom, but this when things can get murky. Even legitimate retailers engage in some spamming practices from time to time. Some buy or rent lists of emails, some acquire them through mergers or bankruptcy liquidations, and some use marketers to aggregate huge lists of potential customers through advanced tracking techniques. Many of these retailers will happily comply with your wish to unsubscribe, but others will take advantage of your request by confirming your email as real and active, making you a perfect target for future spam. Less-than-legitimate marketers have no intention of removing you from any of their mailing lists, so if you do not have a feel for which retailers can be trusted, it's best to simply ignore and delete unwanted solicitations rather than unsubscribing from them. But sometimes a simple Google search for the company or email domain will provide more insight if you're not sure how to proceed.

Filter Out the Junk

Junk or spam email filters are extremely helpful at minimizing those unwanted solicitations that pound users and their PCs daily. These filters operate on both the server level and the local PC or device level within the email software. Server-level filters for email usually apply a simple numeric threshold scale. How much spam can you withstand? Choose "1" to

SENIOR CYBER

allow all messages into your mailbox or choose "10" to filter out every email except those from known senders. Filter scales come in various shapes and sizes, so be sure to consult your internet service provider (ISP) or email provider and be prepared to experiment a little. Everyone's definition of and tolerance for spam is a little different.

Outlook and Apple Mail both include settings for stopping junk mail in its tracks, but there are other applications from third-party developers that go the extra mile at email organization and filtering. Thunderbird, eM Client, and Spike are all free email providers (also programs or applications) that support both Mac and Windows operating systems. Some email services charge money to unlock extra features, but I've been running a business for over twenty years and collaborating with CEOs, engineers, and editors (the very ones from this book) who use the free Apple Mail with no issues, so don't feel like you're missing out on any great email programs if they are free. In the world of smartphones and tablets, these email clients, as well as Edison Mail by Edison Software and MyMail by My.com, can be found easily on any app store to download and try for free.

SECURITY CHALLENGES

When you first set up a new email account, you may be prompted to provide answers to security challenge questions to validate your identity in case you forget your password. Back before social media, this concept made sense. After all, why would anyone but you know which high school you attended, the first concert you ever saw, or your favorite pet's name? But if you've been visiting and posting on social media anytime in the past decade, you will begin to see how answers to questions like these can be easily obtained by anyone.

Unfortunately, many account creations still require some form of antiquated security challenge questions, rather than requiring two-factor authentication, which we previously discussed. However, there's nothing to stop you from providing your own extra layer of security by either creating word associations or giving fake answers only you would know. For instance, since most security challenge questions ask about a school you attended, any run-of-the-mill cyberthief trying to hack your account can simply look up your name and do a "reverse search" for all the schools you attended by using any one of the public or paid school databases available on the internet. So why not respond to that question with the wrong answer when you are first asked? I'm sure you remember the name of a bully who picked on you or the person you had a crush on or the dance where you had your first kiss. Answers to those questions can be found only in your head. By connecting the dots between the original question and the unexpected answer you provide, you are creating an added layer of security that is essentially impenetrable for hackers. That is true security.

 **SENIOR CYBER TIP:** If a website forces you to complete security challenge questions and answers, you don't have to be honest or even make any sense. Try using any old password as an answer to their security challenge question. No hacker would ever guess that the first school you attended was called "Fido1948!."

11

Cautionary Tales

We hear so many stories of hacking and security breaches in the news that it's hard to believe anyone can be trusted. Trust is earned by our friends, family, neighbors, and those we do business with. It can be difficult to trust people we do not know personally, but it's even more difficult to shut out everyone we do not know from our lives, since everyone is a stranger at first. Therefore, it is more important to recognize others' intent rather than just their voice, phone number, or signature, for example. A stranger asking for the time or talking about the weather isn't as much of a threat as an acquaintance asking for your phone's PIN or, even worse, a presumed loved one asking for money in an emergency.

In my first book, *Hacked Again*, I mentioned a popular scam that targets senior citizens, and it bears repeating in this book. Keep a few details in mind before I begin, which might help you spot the scamming methodology as you read along. My nana and papa are both deceased now, but my grandmother lived well into her late eighties, and my grandfather died just shy of his hundredth birthday. At the time of this story, both were active members in their retirement community and were relatively healthy, intelligent, and independent. They had lived in a large assisted-living complex for over fifteen hundred seniors. One weekend night, they received an urgent phone call on their landline that my grandfather answered.

"Grandpa, it's me. I am in trouble and up in Canada," a young male voice called out over a weak phone connection.

"Who is this?" Papa asked.

"It's me, your grandchild," the person responded.

"Brian? Is that you?" Papa exclaimed.

"Yes," the caller replied. "I need help. I drove up to Canada with some friends for a fishing trip, but they had drugs in the car, and we all got arrested."

My grandfather didn't know what to do, but he knew this was no time for a lecture or scolding; it seemed like an emergency.

"I need you to send me ten thousand dollars immediately so that they'll drop the charges and let me out of jail," the voice confessed. "Please, the money must be received tonight before they close because there will be no way to get it tomorrow—it's Sunday," he continued.

Papa worriedly replied, "Okay, how do I do that?"

"Go quickly to the nearest Staples store, get a wire transfer document, and transfer the funds to this account number from your bank immediately," the voice instructed. "But don't wait, because if you don't do it now, they will keep me locked up all weekend and might not even drop the charges. And whatever you do, don't tell my mom," he finished.

Papa hung up the phone, grabbed Nana, and explained the situation to her on the way to Staples. There was a Staples store located conveniently across the street, and as they entered, the two made a beeline over to the customer support counter to inquire about sending money via wire transfer. As they waited in line, a cashier overheard them talking.

"Do you mind me asking who you are trying to wire transfer funds to?" she asked my grandparents.

They told her all about their grandson's call and the details of his story. The cashier told them both to stop and think, because there had been several other seniors in the store earlier that day with a similar story. This gave them pause, and they decided to call their grandson Brian directly to be sure it was really him, even though Papa insisted the caller sounded just like him. They called Brian and immediately learned he was not in Canada or in jail but rather in Georgia, where he lived. Nana and Papa felt embarrassed but relieved. Did you pick up on some of the clues indicating this was the work of hackers specifically targeting seniors?

The hacker called on a landline. Unlike cell phones, most landline phones are not configured to provide caller ID before you answer. The hacker also used a landline to disguise their specific vocal characteristics over a distant and weak phone connection, supposedly coming from Canada. Compared to the high fidelity of most digital smartphones today, old landlines leave a lot to be desired in terms of audio quality. Elderly ears sometimes hear what they want to hear, so a troubled young male voice could sound just like the voice of a grandson who might be inclined to get himself into trouble. Since many grandparents have multiple grandsons, it's just a matter of letting the senior victim identify the specific grandson by name before offering any more information. From there, the hacker is relying on a past history they couldn't possibly know but that a concerned grandparent is more than willing to share and ruminate about.

Whether the communication is through a text message, voicemail, email, or phone call, the hacker's tempo is always hurried. The scenario is usually an emergency and must be addressed before time runs out. Of course, there is no real dilemma, but the scammer is still in the driver's seat at this point. There were other tell-tale details to indicate this was a scam that my grandparents missed.

The hacker called my grandfather by the generic title of *Grandpa*. Most adult grandchildren I know still call their grandparents by the same cute nicknames they did as young children. Some go by Gramps and Granny, Oma and Opa, Baba and Gigi, Mawmaw and Pawpaw. Every sibling, cousin, nephew, and niece I grew up with called my grandparents Nana and Papa for as long as I can remember. If Papa hadn't been so trusting and concerned with the hacker's story, he would've picked up on it.

Another suspicious detail is the fact that the hacker named Staples by name. Of course, it could have been a coincidence, but to name a retail store that is also the only one within walking distance from the target's home raises a red flag for me. When small details like these begin to add up, it's time to turn the tables on the scammer. There is nothing wrong with asking a few pointed questions when you know you are speaking with a loved one, so why not ask some questions if you are not entirely sure? Don't be intimidated into silence, and don't be rushed into *any* action. This same advice also applies to telemarketers, spammers, and long-lost friends, not just criminals.

FOREWARNED IS FOREARMED

Here are a few stages of response you can try if you find yourself in a situation you think might be a scam:

1. Tell the person on the other end of the line that you have an emergency and need to call them right back. Ask for the number. If they do not immediately reply with a phone number, you can bet they are not telling you the entire story.

2. If they do provide you with a number, you now have the upper hand. You can Google that number and see if it is associated with any scams that others have reported. Just type in the number and words like "scam," "fraud," "criminal," and perhaps a few words that relate directly to their story. Don't get too bogged down in the details of their story, as the names, places, and dates will always be adjusted slightly.

3. If you do not see any search results that resemble their phone number or their story, don't worry, because you still have the upper hand. You are no longer on the spot and being prodded to make snap decisions. You can concentrate on their words and the consequences of action versus inaction on your part. The popular game show *Who Wants to Be a Millionaire* allowed contestants to phone a friend for answers, so why not give someone you trust a call before making any decisions? They might not see right through the scammer's lies, but it can help to have an extra brain when running through a problem.

I'm not advocating being rude or lying to anyone, especially if they are truly in distress and need your help, but taking control is just another aspect of being an informed consumer and vital member of a community. By not falling prey to scammers, and by reporting them to authorities, you are acting not only as a neighborhood watch but also an internet watchdog. Visit websites like www.scam.com for a full directory of known scams organized by categories, dates, and number of user reports. You can peruse the directory if you enjoy reading stories like these, and you can post your own encounter with a scammer to help warn others.

ADVANCED SCAMMERS

Scammers and hackers live on the cutting edge of technology. They are always trying to leverage the latest tactics and technologies against their targets. As a cybersecurity expert, keeping up with their latest exploits is a full-time job, so by the time I factor in my family life, writings, and side projects, and running my own forty-eight-year-old family business, it's hard to stay on top of the latest scams. I was recently approached by CBS News to help investigate a diabolical new scheme and will share some details with you to help underline the point that *you can never be too careful.*

In this particular story, a woman's bank contacted her with a fraud alert via text message. Before she could even react, she received a phone call informing her of some fraudulent activity details on her account, including a withdrawal of $2,700. The operator already knew her name, address, and last four digits of her bank card, and the woman was told to freeze the account to avoid further theft. The voice on the other end of the line even told this woman to verify her bank's phone and, sure enough, the caller ID on her phone not only displayed the number and name of her bank but the same phone number listed on the bank's website. The operator then transferred her to an automated line that would take her PIN code to verify her identity and proceed with the card freeze. At that point, the woman had no reason to doubt the caller's identity or suggestions, so she entered her PIN code. I must admit that I might have acted similarly.

So what were some of the warning signs? The target's name, phone number, address, and even the last four digits of her bank card are readily available for about fifteen dollars on the Dark Web, but what about the caller ID verification? How did the caller manage to spoof her bank's real phone number? After some research, I learned about several free apps available to anyone who wants to hide their identity. Just like it's legal to use an unlisted number, it's also technically legal to spoof other phone numbers and names through caller ID. These apps and services exist primarily to protect the identities of parties with sensitive or private information, but that doesn't stop hackers from abusing these apps for their own scams.

When I presented my findings to CBS, the producers wanted to shoot a live demonstration of the technology. So I did more research and found a free app that allowed me to easily create any phone number I wanted to display (real or not) along with a custom name or company or message. Sure enough, even with all the AI smarts of my iPhone, I was still able to fool it into showing that my dog was calling me from my wife's phone.

This is one instance in which the internet and search engines can provide a false sense of security or, in this case, identity. Once a scammer has earned a victim's trust, they can either request more information or choose to go in for the kill. All they really needed to make a quick, unauthorized withdrawal from the woman's account was her PIN code. It helps to know, however, that real customer service personnel are generally not authorized to ask for personal security information, such as passwords or PIN codes, over the phone. So to circumvent the likelihood she might refuse, they cleverly transferred her over to a touchtone receiver that instantly translated the audible tones into a series of numbers that compromised her PIN code.

I have no doubt that within minutes of receiving this PIN code, the scammers had already withdrawn as much money as they could in one transaction. As it turned out, once the woman finally got in touch with her real bank, she learned that the scammers stole $2,300. Fortunately, her bank eventually agreed to reimburse her for the loss, but when all of those verifiable details were used against her, how could this hack have been avoided?

Turning the Tables on Spoofers

In this particular scam, the thieves successfully managed to fool the victim by posing as a believable and proactive security fraud department of a real bank. If you've ever dealt with credit fraud departments, you will see both similarities and differences among banks. Try to keep a rough idea of their protocols and requests in mind next time you receive an email, text, or phone call from your bank. Most banks and credit unions, especially regional ones, have their own unique approach to fraud investigation and customer support. You might even recognize the voice of a specific operator, language of an email, or twang of an accent. Little clues like these can help alert you to potential scams.

If you feel something might be amiss, question the person trying to get you to take some action you may not be comfortable with. A legitimate representative will have a good answer that makes sense—and remember, once you have verified your identity, no additional verification is needed for the duration of the interaction. If they ask for more, press them on their needs and do not be afraid to simply hang up.

Most of this scam's success can be ascribed to its sense of urgency. The bank appeared to be proactive by texting and then immediately following up with a phone call, *but* if your bank has never done those types of things in the past, that might raise your suspicions. In any case, by being proactive, the scammers' goal was to put their victim on the spot. She felt forced to answer the criminal's questions quickly before even more damage could be done to her account, but if she had simply called them back, she would've completely turned the tables on them. By hang-ing up and visiting the bank's website or just looking at the back of her bank card for a phone number, the victim would have resumed control by dialing the real bank directly. The scammers would have given up on her and moved on to the next victim.

12

The Nature of the Security Biz

Hacks and theft are hard to trace, enabling cybercriminals to move freely around the internet, Dark Web, and of course, the real world. For every thousand attempts to steal, blackmail, or attack a victim, hackers need to fool only one victim and then cover their own tracks. They have millions of potential targets and lots of time to perfect their malware and scams. Proving a digital currency theft took place is hard enough, but proving who did it is nearly impossible.

As a cybersecurity expert, my goal is to help others avoid hackers and their crimes. This begins by shoring up my own defenses and avoiding the scams and pitfalls myself. But just because I can evade a dangerous hack does not mean I can stop it from happening to anyone else. I can only pass on the knowledge to readers, viewers, and visitors to my website and hope they are paying attention.

Contrary to popular movies and novels that sometimes glamorize the hacker culture, cyber-security is all about the low-hanging fruit. Small businesses do not have the resources to fight attacks and always prevent breaches. Consumers do not have the wherewithal to defend their private data from an onslaught of hackers. And, unfortunately, seniors are among the easiest of the low-hanging fruit to pick and offer the biggest payouts for cyber-criminals. Many seniors are also confused or embarrassed by being ripped off by some computer-savvy kids halfway around the world. They often do not report the criminal action, partly because they're humiliated and partly because they don't even know whom to call. Cyber insurance and cybersecurity services are offered only to high-powered executives and their giant corporations, not our elders. Cyber help for seniors typically comes from a family member or trusted friend who is knowledgeable enough to install the right software while keeping a watchful eye out for malware on their family's computers. Couple that with the fact that many seniors feel as if technology has passed them by. They are frustrated the world won't slow down enough for them to enjoy the wonders of technology.

THERE OUGHT TO BE A LAW

I cannot remember a time when so many politicians, who normally disagree with each other, have come together and agree on one thing: regulation is necessary. Many Americans believe certain tech giants have grown too large to maintain so much personal data safely, and if those companies continue to go unchecked, that will lead to global ruination. The majority of both Democrats and Republicans seem to agree that some form of government regulation is needed to keep giant social networks like Google, Facebook, and Twitter in check. Many legislators also believe we face threats from Chinese tech giants that have also infiltrated our devices, culture, and lives. Of course, each side seems to have its own motives and approaches to the problem, but it's still good to see the potential for bipartisan legislation afoot.

In April 2016, the European Union (EU) managed to pass General Data Protection Regulation (GDPR), which affects much more than just the EU. After all, once we all become connected, we should also agree to common standards and laws. GDPR gives individuals control over their personal data and how it's used, the regulatory environment is simplified, and companies that violate the law are heavily fined. And when I say "heavily fined," I mean it literally. Fines can reach up to 4 percent of a company's annual gross revenue. So rather than the paltry multimillion-dollar slap on the wrist most tech companies have received, they are now looking at a *multibillion-dollar* smack on the wrist. While GDPR will not magically fix our country's cyber problems, it's still real legislation that has gone into effect, which is much more than the US Congress has done to ensure our cybersafety.

The Battle over Net Neutrality

As we enter the 2020s, the same country that created the internet and the biggest tech companies in history has yet to implement federal laws to protect its citizens' digital

privacy and security. Telecom and ISP companies are given free rein to deliver some of the
slowest internet speeds to mostly rural and
poor communities—all under the guise of "free
market competition." Those same companies
also maintain monopolies over many regions,
often giving consumers only one choice for their
internet, TV, and phone bundles.

 SENIOR CYBER TIP: Net neutrality
is the principle that internet service
providers should enable the same
access to *all* content, regardless of
source, without favoring or blocking any
particular site for any reason.

Regulatory agencies like the FCC seem
content to let giant telecoms duke it out with
it each other at the expense of smaller telecoms and millions of neglected customers.
The current FCC chairman, Ajit Pai, claims
the agency wants only to stimulate competition—but at what cost is he willing to let

these companies set their own agendas? Protections like net neutrality are designed to treat all data and *customers* the same, but the FCC viewed this safeguard as a (supposed) hindrance to free market competition, so the proposal enacted in 2015 was dismantled by a 3–2 vote in 2017.[15] As a result, we're beginning to see telecom giants bundle proprietary content and services so no customer will be able to watch their favorite program without subscribing to an expensive bundle of services from the only provider in their area. Free market competition begins with freedom of choice, neither of which benefit any of the monopolistic giants.

---

15 Andrew Soergel, "FCC Votes to Dismantle Obama-Rea Net Neutrality Standards," USNews, December 14, 2017, https://www.usnews.com/news/economy/articles/2017-12-14/fcc-votes-to-dismantle-obama-era-net-neutrality-standards.

THE PARTY LINE

On the one hand, we have a Republican-led FCC that champions a free and open internet by reducing regulations, but on the other hand, the current Republican majority in the US Senate champions regulation of social media networks. To confuse matters further, the same group of politicians and pundits (and even the US president himself) want social media companies to run unimpeded by government interference. However, they also complain that conservative views and groups are being unfairly attacked on those same media platforms and even tried to ban the social media video site TikTok. They can't have it both ways.

These contradictory stances from the same party are by no means the only examples of this hypocrisy. The majority of Democrats seem hell-bent on defending all forms of free speech except fake political ads and hate speech. Of course, the fake political ads tend to favor Republican candidates, so there is a clear bias shaping Democratic opinions and proposed legislation.

It's a Jungle Out There

Jobs have always been a major campaign issue, and the most recent elections are no exception. With many manufacturing jobs lost to automation and China, the big tech industry has been making inroads into more major US cities. You may recall Amazon's public bid to build a second headquarters in a major US city. It floated the idea in front of the world to see which cities would line up to offer it the most incentives in return for some twenty-five thousand jobs. In 2019, New York's Long Island City seemed to be a shoo-in for the newly proposed HQ2 until the state's progressive Democrats challenged Amazon's plans by asking why Amazon should receive $3.5 billion in tax incentives when the company hadn't paid any income tax at all in recent years.[16]

Amid that political pressure, Amazon pulled out of the deal at the last minute, leaving politicians on both sides of the aisle pointing fingers in every direction. Since everyone values employment opportunities, the idea of turning away so many potential

16 Jacob Kastrenakes, "Amazon Cancels HQ2 in New York After Backlash," The Verge, February 14, 2019, https://www.theverge.com/2019/2/14/18224993/amazon-hq-2-queens-new-york-backlash-pulls-drops.

jobs seemed foolish, but on the other hand, it became clear that Amazon was simply playing cities against each other and the tax system against itself to secure billions of dollars in free incentives without offering anything (other than the promise of jobs) in return. While it's not illegal to play hopeful municipalities off of one another, it did leave a bad taste in every taxpayer's mouth, especially considering the company had just been valued at $1 trillion.

The only clear winners in these scenarios seem to be the large companies. Every corporation needs to run a tight ship and make cuts where needed, but nearly every Fortune 500 company is breaking all kinds of revenue and profit records while the federal and state governments are starved for larger tax revenues. Adding more laws and beneficiaries of the state hasn't worked out too well in the past, but we are living in different times now. The left is looking more to the EU as a model for financial stability, while the right seems content in letting big corporations and free market competition handle it themselves.

Whichever side you fall on, you do have a voice. FCC Chairman Ajit Pai was appointed to the FCC by President Obama and then appointed as the FCC chairman by President Trump, so the entire country's vote plays a role in the FCC and its stance on important issues like net neutrality. As for jobs, free speech, and data privacy, all US legislators face removal when enough Americans vote to replace them, so it's better to become fully informed before pulling the lever. I recommend perusing tech websites like www.theverge.com, www.wired.com, and www.mashable.com for an even mix of technology and culture news and how that affects our daily lives.

VOTING WITH YOUR WALLET

Successful political movements involving public busing in Montgomery, Alabama, the National Farm Workers Association, and ending apartheid in South Africa all required sustained momentum and economic boycott. Most boycotts are both ineffective and misunderstood. Boycotts are large, organized groups of people who stop frequenting establishments or purchasing products from specific companies or regions to force change through political and economic pressure.

Refusing to go to McDonald's for oversalting your fries doesn't constitute a genuine boycott. In an instance like that, you are simply exercising your consumer-purchasing muscle; but you are only one person, and McDonald's won't miss your business. If "boycotting" McDonald's makes you feel good, then do it. Citizens should never be lulled into inaction and neither should consumers, but there is a distinct difference between political boycotts that protect civil rights and consumer choice, which preserves competition among companies.

If you're interested in starting or joining a movement to pressure Amazon into paying its fair share of federal taxes, or perhaps you want to keep Facebook free of censorship, there are many ways to get the word out. However, according to most activist organi-zations, simply signing an online petition or retweeting a powerful quote is never enough. Face-to-face remains the strongest method of activism and leads to the greatest change. However, tremendous social and economic change can be spawned from the internet—as it did in the case of the Muslim protests against oppressive regimes in the early 2010s, called the Arab Spring—but the number of online protests that quickly lose steam far outnumber movements that go the distance. So what's an activist to do?

SEARCHING IS YOUR FRIEND

The internet is vast and populated with opinions. If you've got a bee in your bonnet about anything, you can bet someone else out there has that same bee buzzing around too. Search engines like Google are your biggest ally initially. Notice I said *initially*, and I'll get back to that in a moment, but first, simply type in the phrase or keywords to find the best match of websites or news stories you are looking for. If you don't see what you want right away, don't worry. Keep searching past the first page of results or try entering some different keywords. Remember, the little guys don't always have the resources to keep up with the latest search algorithms, so their websites might not appear at the top of the list. They also don't have the money to spend on advertising, so you won't find activism sites on the right side of the page where paid ads often reside.

What's the Downside?

However, search engines can begin to lead you off the beaten path at this point, and they are also where things can get dicey. Over the years, Google has been accused of playing favorites with their advertisers, including unfair promotion of stories that portray them and their partners in a favorable light. Google has also faced some heavy fines, paid them, and continued to proclaim its innocence. Of course, the claims of innocence are deeply tied to Google's search algorithms, which remain closely guarded secrets, so it remains difficult to ascertain the company's innocence, much less all its motives.

Given the consolidation, merging, and buyouts among tech companies, the notion of boycotting is almost quaint if not downright impossible. When your only search engine is Google, or your only source for shopping is Amazon, or every computer you encounter runs Microsoft, or all of your personal devices are made by Apple, do you really have much choice? Well, you do always have a choice, but it's a matter of framing your choices to maintain communication in this modern age. What are your priorities? Security? Consumer choice? Free speech? As they say, pick your battles wisely.

13

In Sickness and
in Health

Ransomware attacks on the healthcare industry saw a 350 percent increase in the fourth quarter of 2019.[17] While there have been an unusually high number of cybersecurity challenges for consumers, companies, and entire industries, healthcare was hit

---

17 *HIPPA Journal,* "Q3, 2019 Saw a 350% Increase in Ransomware Attacks on Healthcare Providers," March 10, 2020, https://www.hipaa-journal.com/q3-2019-saw-a-350-increase-in-ransomware-attacks-on-healthcare-providers/.

particularly hard on both the practitioner and patient sides.

> **SENIOR CYBER TIP: Ransomware** is a type of malware that infects a computer and restricts all access to it until the user pays a demanded ransom, usually in an anonymous digital payment, such as Bitcoin.

Entire hospitals, staffs, and patients have been held hostage while greedy hackers demand payment to release data from computer networks. A recent article reports that 41 percent of the US population has had their healthcare records exposed, disclosed without permission, or outright stolen by hackers.[18]

As of this writing, the COVID-19 virus has infected millions, killed hundreds of thousands,

---

18 Darina Lynkova, "23+ Staggering Healthcare Data Breach Statistics in 2020," Leftronic, October 25, 2019, https://leftronic.com/healthcare-data-breach-statistics/.

and continues to spread in every corner of the globe. Much like influenza, it appears COVID-19 will become even more widespread once the next flu season begins, and it's proven particularly dangerous to those suffering from weakened immune systems.

THE GOOD NEWS AND THE BAD NEWS

I'm not trying to scare you into inactivity but rather to become more proactive. Consumers, especially seniors, should be actively on guard against healthcare scams. The elderly and immunocompromised populations are ultrasensitive to medical cures, claims, and remedies and are thus targeted even more by cybercriminals. These criminals might pretend to be doctors, but the scams are more likely to take the form of spam or infomercials that play on the fears and hopes of their audience. However, there is one big difference between passive TV, radio, and postal messages and interactive platforms, including social media, email, and videoconferencing: we can easily turn off an annoying TV commercial, but it's not so easy to turn off a spammer, especially if you've already clicked on the email. They will keep pounding your email inbox with new pills and tonics because they know you are interested. You are a captive audience, as they say in the media business. And even if you *didn't* click, these scammers can simply change their messaging until eventually you do. The same holds true with "likes" on social media or responding to any suspicious text messages. *Never* click on or reply to any message you were not expecting from someone you do not know.

During the initial COVID-19 pandemic, in early

to mid-2020, many users flocked to videoconferencing platforms, such as FaceTime, Skype, and Zoom, to communicate with loved ones or work remotely in a time of crisis. Hackers also flocked to the same digital conversations, but for very different reasons. As a result, many videoconferences were subjected to pornography, hate speech, and general mayhem by hackers interrupting connections that users believed to be private and secure. It became clear that many of our videoconferencing platforms did not foresee Zoom-bombing, as it has come to be known. Even the FBI has publicly warned users about this practice.

 **SENIOR CYBER TIP: Zoom-bombing** is the term that describes uninvited guests who join, intercept, or spam a private video conversation.

Like photobombing—meaning unwanted people who purposefully jump into your pictures just as you take them—Zoom-bombing is mostly

harmless pranking, but it could lead to harass-
ment, bullying, and further targeted hacking.
When someone invades our physical or digital
space without consent, it can feel very threat-
ening and lead to social withdrawal for many.
That is why it is important to follow basic security protocols when hosting or joining any video
chat, even if it's with just one other person.

Videoconferencing via the Zoom platform
became hugely popular during the epidemic
because it allowed up to one hundred users
to simultaneously video chat and also because
no account or password creations were initially
required; anyone could use it at any time. Origi-
nally created for virtual business meetings, Zoom
was quickly adopted by millions of people looking
to chat with family and friends, so the software
quickly showed its deficits in some areas. By
default, all Zoom virtual meetings were public
and unlocked. This made Zoom easy to use, but
as we've previously discussed, the more convenient things are, the less secure they become.

In the real world, if someone wanted to

interrupt a small conference in a building, they would have to travel to the building, find the room number, and hope the doors aren't locked and no invitations are required for entry. With Zoom (and other less-secure videoconferencing software), those barriers were removed. Finding the meeting location was as simple as asking someone for the meeting number or letting computer software automatically guess the meeting number.

Many of those security shortcomings have been addressed by Zoom and other videoconferencing software since the outbreak, but I still would not recommend them over more secure platforms, such as Apple's FaceTime and Google's Hangouts. Those platforms allow dozens of simultaneous participants, and, more important, they cull the list from your known contacts so no strangers can invade your private chats.

The Good, the Bad, and the Ugly

As COVID-19 continued to spread, along with fake news and hysteria, scammers took note and joined the plague of disinformation. With so much information flying about, it became nearly impossible to sort through all of the data, which I've labeled the good, the bad, and the ugly.

Good, truthful information comes from trusted, well-known sources, like the federal, local, or state governments, as well as large corporations and organizations. These sources might not always be 100 percent correct, but they have all the resources and incentives in the world to spread helpful and factual information.

Bad information can be well-meaning but misinformed. This misinformation comes from a place of sharing but does not adhere to any scientific standards or cross-referenced, peer-reviewed sources. This information might have an agenda, but it's usually so focused on stoking the fears inherent to that agenda that the safety and health of others isn't important. "Bad actors" might be loved ones or social media groups that forward COVID-19 links and stories without vetting them at all or a company selling expensive face masks that do not adequately protect users from virulent particles.

The *ugly* information floating around is intentionally false and simply profits from suffering. Users searching for medical remedies are lured in by the false claims; money and/or private information can be stolen from them, and no medicine is delivered at all. During the initial stages of the COVID-19 outbreak, cybersecurity analysts saw a spike in ransomware attacks on hospitals and testing centers. Emails and robocalls claiming to offer medical treatments and donations to the sick increased significantly during that time. These are all scams and should be not only ignored but prosecuted for theft of money and resources from the real heroes and victims of COVID-19. Even the FTC and FCC could no longer turn their backs on robocall abuse. Both government departments issued severe warnings to any gateway VoIP ("voice over IP" uses internet protocols to transmit and receive voice communications) company that did not block all COVID-19-related robocalls of overseas origins within forty-eight hours. You have to wonder why they could not simply require identification and blocking of all *other* scamming robocalls, too, but at least it's a start.

GOVERNMENT ISSUED

Seniors have a particular set of priorities when compared with the rest of the population. They typically rely on their Social Security checks, their Medicare and Medicaid assistance, and their social groups consisting of family and friends—which is *precisely* why hackers can target seniors successfully. Letters, emails, and phone messages purporting to be from the IRS, Social Security Administration, and publicly assisted healthcare programs would be ignored by most younger and middle-aged people, but seniors who rely on those services know how important it is to cross every *t* and dot every *i* when it comes to government forms and benefits.

If told even a tiny possibility existed that you might not receive your monthly check, you would probably reply to a message claiming there was a mistake or problem with that check. I'm not saying there's anything wrong with following up on those types of details, but I am telling you there is a safe and secure way to do so.

Never reply to any email or phone message directly by using the included link or return phone number. Look at your existing paperwork or past records to find the known, safe phone number or link, or simply type in www.irs.gov, for example. All official government websites end with a .gov and include safe access agents, departments, or documents. If someone claiming to be from your local bank contacts you, do your due diligence before getting back to them. If you were expecting their call or their message wasn't a surprise, then gather your paperwork, as always, and reach out to the company yourself for more information. But if their question or message caught you off guard, then get back on guard.

For instance, the Medicare.gov website has an entire section dedicated to helping seniors identify and prevent potential scams. Part of the advice includes: "Guard your Medicare card like it's a credit card. Remember:

- Medicare will never contact you for your Medicare number or other personal information unless you've given them permission in advance.
- Medicare will never call you to sell you anything.
- You may get calls from people promising you things if you give them a Medicare number. Don't do it.
- Medicare will never visit you at your home.
- Medicare can't enroll you over the phone unless you called first."[19]

---

19 "Help Fight Medicare Fraud," Medicare.gov, accessed July 1, 2020, https://www.medicare.gov/forms-help-resources/help-fight-medicare-fraud.

Never offer your full account number or Social Security or credit card numbers to any institution, including your own bank. They might ask you to provide partial numbers to prove your identity, but they already have those full numbers. So if you are ever asked to provide full account numbers, simply explain that you are uncomfortable with providing that information and ask for an alternative way to prove your identity. If the call is from a legitimate bank or institution, you will be asked to prove your identity by another method, such as your last deposit amount and date. If the caller is not who they claim to be, get prepared for them to spin a story to convince you otherwise, or they will just hang up.

If the caller insists you contact them, call or write to them *only* through the proper channels. Do not reply to an unknown email or phone number. Rather, use the methods that have worked well in the past or, better yet, go to the official website or past correspondence to work your way through the departments.

Saving a few minutes of waiting on hold is nothing compared to the headache you will save by preventing a hack or scam.

14

Avoiding the "Con" in Confidence

We have all received our share of unsolic-ited phone calls, emails, and even visits to our home, but these unsolicited contacts, while probably annoying, are not the same as targeted scams. By bringing us all a little closer together, the internet has also enabled the world's largest collection of intimate facts about you, me, and nearly everyone else on the planet. For a price, marketers, politicians, and companies can buy their way into your life with targeted advertising campaigns. Since one cannot expect to remain completely private while on the internet, this is more of an invasion of seclusion rather than an invasion of privacy, but it's no less disrupting. And while these targeted campaigns are normally legal, they can easily be abused and twisted into something altogether different and downright scary.

Long before the days of automated data mining by big tech companies, con men (short for confidence men) would research their marks (victims) meticulously and calculate the best way to sell their wares or just flat-out steal from the unsuspecting targets. One of the con man's most powerful tactics is to make their marks feel like it's their own idea to invest in something with a huge potential upside. This method leverages the victim's ego against their own self-interest and further establishes trust in the relationship. I've seen these "cons" illustrated well in many films and TV programs, but it's particularly upsetting when it happens in real life to a loved one.

These days, investors who get in on the ground floor of new investments early are sometimes called angel investors. This designation sounds harmless and pumps up the ego of any investor who might consider themselves brilliant for saving a nascent technology or inventor from financial ruin. However, angel investing is just another label for both good and bad investments, so as I always recommend, proceed with caution.

Throughout his life, my grandfather was a shrewd investor. He never gambled savings away on long-shot investments. Besides long-term ownership of a few institutional stocks, such as AT&T and IBM, he used the majority of his savings to reinvest back into his family in the form of education, real estate, and leisure pursuits. He remained lucid and skeptical into his nineties, but once my grandmother and his wife of seventy-one years died, he became someone who craved his privacy while also reaching out to others for solace and comfort. Unfortunately, strangers were more than happy to step into these roles and brought with them supposed "once-in-a-life-time" investment opportunities. Of course, these opportunities were couched as friendly voices over the phone that lavished praise on my grandfather for being such a wise inves-tor. My grandfather would occasionally recount stories in which the anonymous brokers would refer to him like a member of their own family. Naturally, we were all concerned, but there is only so much one can do to stop a grown man with his own resources and independence.

One day while visiting, my father intercepted a phone call from a broker who was urging my grandfather to stop selling so many stock shares at a loss. Apparently, my grandfather was following terrible advice from an internet stock market prognosticator who claimed the entire market was overdue for a crash and that everyone should jump ship before it was too late. He listened to that huckster's advice while ignoring repeated warnings from his own broker to stop selling valuable positions at a loss. To make matters worse, the funds from some of those valuable stocks were then invested back into high-risk ventures that were not publicly traded or under the scrutiny of the Securities and Exchange Commission (SEC). These privately funded companies included things like oil wells in Texas and miracle drugs that had not run through any clinical trials or testing. None of them included any provisions for dividend payouts or shareholder voting rights. The only guarantee seemed to be the inevitable shakedown for even more money from investors to pump up the stock.

So how did such a once shrewd investor and lifelong engineer like my grandfather fall prey to fraudulent investment scams? There is no single reason, but I suspect his age made him more vulnerable to the hype that promised outlandish returns. As a resident of an assisted living community, he was bombarded with phone calls, emails, and physical mailings all tuned into his potential wealth, health, and investment inclinations. These solicitations were not wide nets cast over him and all of his neighbors but rather focused initiatives. They were similar to targeted hacking attacks like "spear phishing."

 SENIOR CYBER TIP: Spear phishing is a targeted attack against an individual by sending fraudulent emails that appear to be from a known or trusted source in order to persuade them into revealing confidential information. There are other forms of phishing attacks that target even more or less specifically than spear phishing, but they all count on unsuspecting users to let down their guard.

Instead of trying to hack his account, these duplicitous marketers tried (and mostly succeeded) to hack his intentions. They used data collected through many websites and services about Bill Schober to spin an attractive message that he would likely respond to and act on. A time limit was put on the offer to encourage him to "get in on the ground floor" before he could think it through. Surely, the marketers also took into account his recent status as a widower, his investment preferences, and his neighbors' preferences, as well. After all, if you've never heard of Company X but your neighbors have, it must be legitimate, right? Today's digital marketers have access to data that marketers from ten years ago could have only dreamed of possessing. An already uneven playing field has been tilted to further exploit his and his neighbors' fears and fragility. The marketers went even further by talking him through their investment schemes over the phone. One hand stroked his ego while the other comforted his trusting heart.

You might think that I'm simply complaining about marketing in general, because all marketers behave in a similar manner, but you would be mistaken. In a 2018 report created by the Federal Trade Commission (FTC) for

Congress called *Protecting Older Consumers*,[20] these were just some of the key findings:

- In 2018, older adults were still the least likely of any age group to report money lost due to fraud, but their individual median dollar losses remained higher than for younger adults.
- Compared to 2017 numbers, reported median individual losses among consumers aged sixty and over increased, and the increase was particularly large for those aged eighty and over.
- Older adults were much more likely than younger consumers to report money lost on tech support scams, prizes, sweepstakes and lottery scams, and family and friend impersonation.
- Phone scams were the most lucrative

---

20 Federal Trade Commission, *Protecting Older Consumers 2018-2019: A Report of the Federal Trade Commission*, October 18, 2019, https://www.ftc.gov/system/files/documents/reports/protecting-older-consumers-2018-2019-report-federal-trade-commission/p144401_protecting_older_consumers_2019_1.pdf.

against older consumers in terms of aggregate losses, and online scams were a distant second.

Make no mistake, seniors are being targeted and ripped off at alarmingly high rates, but they are not helpless. Any senior can take steps to stay safe, and if they cannot do it themselves, a partner or trusted friend or family member can do it for them. This book is full of tips, but here are a few key points to avoid investment fraud:

- If you feel pressure to act on an offer, stop and take the time to check it out.
- Most investment opportunities are registered with your state's securities regulator or the SEC. If an opportunity is not registered, then it's probably not legitimate. Visit www.nasaa.org to find and contact your state regulator.
- Do not respond to any phone calls, emails, or texts from people you don't already know. If you do, the scammers

will put you on their potential investor lists regardless of how you respond.

- If you use a stockbroker or investment adviser, check the Central Registration Depository (CRD) or Form ADV, respectively, for possible complaints and violations associated with them. Form ADV is the uniform form used by investment advisers to register with both the SEC and state securities authorities. Visit www.finra.org/BrokerCheck to research suspicious brokers, advisers, and firms.

- Search Google for any contact information or investment opportunities presented to you. If the person scammed someone in the past, you can probably learn more about it on the internet.

- Visit www.investor.gov and www.nasaa.org/investor-education for alerts about recent investment scams, and also visit www.aarp.org/money/scams-fraud/ to learn more investor protection tips.

15

Preparing for the Worst

We can beat back hackers and data thieves by using best security practices, but death is not preventable. Death steals from everyone, but that doesn't mean it has to make life harder on the living. Only a small percentage of people actually die unexpectedly, so preliminary end-of-life preparations are vital for families. This can include a last will and testament, funeral preparations, or even legal gatherings called to tie up loose ends. But since we all live in a digital world, those loose ends now extend far beyond a lifetime. Remember, in the digital age, caretaking goes far beyond the natural lifespan of someone and even beyond their estate. The internet has given us all the power of true legacy, so that legacy must be protected by loved ones and family.

Before discussing the details, make sure you and your loved ones are on the same page about your final wishes and stewardship duties. There might not be as much legalese or paperwork involved, but stewardship of care roles can be much more complex and fraught with emotional pitfalls than a typical arrangement.

Start by making lists. Take your time and jot down every account, service, subscription, log-in information, personal contact, etc., you can think of, especially the reoccurring ones. As long as your smartphones and computers are backed up on a separate device or to the cloud, all you really need are the log-in names and passwords to access most of this information. Still, you'd be amazed by how difficult it can be to find those old emails or text messages when you need them most, so there's no time like the present. Make one column for yourself and one shared column that you and your loved one(s), family member(s), or friend(s) might contribute to. If you have a spouse or partner, make sure they do the same to compare notes, and help each other if need be.

THE POWER OF LISTS

My grandparents passed away recently, but they had moved into an assisted living facility about fifteen years ago. At the time they moved into their retirement community, they had no outstanding health issues and were happy to live out the rest of their lives with each other. And even though their plan went more or less as predicted, they didn't hesitate to share all vital information with each other as soon as they moved into the complex in the event one of them forgot or lost the ability to communicate details later. They wrote down plenty of account numbers, names, phone numbers, and notes for each other, and I recommend the same for anyone else in that position. In fact, these lists of crucial details and instructions should be revisited annually as the list of services expands. Don't rely on memory, and don't wait to write things down. Pick an anniversary date—or maybe when you do your taxes—and make that the same time you also go over your log-ins, websites, and apps list each year. Update that list with your partner or designated friend or family member to keep everyone informed and up to date.

I recommend you treat your data the same way you treat your financials and healthcare. If you have access to a safe or safety deposit box, be sure to write down emails, usernames, and passwords used for every log-in and store them in a safe place. Better yet, create a hard copy on a typewriter or computer and print it out. I have trouble reading my own handwriting, so I can imagine the difficulty in trying to guess something written in another's handwriting.

Next, catalog every payment method you use, including credit and debit cards, savings and checking accounts, and online payment services, such as PayPal, Venmo, Stripe, and Square. Make sure you also include access to your banking, stocks and bonds, IRAs, 401(k)s, Social Security and Medicare log-ins, insurance policies, and any other investment portfolios that can accrue over a lifetime. Finally, you must list the pertinent information for all of your current websites (think social media and other personal-use sites), utilities, and subscriptions.

It's important to remember that cataloging this information is about much more than money. Cancelling a deceased loved one's credit cards and closing their accounts must be done in order to avoid basic fraud and theft, but keeping passwords and identity credentials safe is a job that continues long after you and your loved ones have passed. Some shared and unique accounts can operate only with the deceased's email address or cell number, so these things might need to remain active long after the funeral and until a proper transition over to the new owner can take place. Keep in mind, if the deceased subscribed to many delivery, entertainment, and transportation services in the form of apps or websites, it might take some time to cancel all of them, but it's worth chasing each one down. Even if you already canceled all the payment methods for those subscriptions, the sites will still retain their subscribers' personal data. If stolen and sold years later, that same data can be used to unlock many other accounts and do some real damage or even theft. Be sure to fully cancel membership to each of these services.

POTENTIAL FOR IDENTITY THEFT

Identity theft is a big enough problem for the living, and it can be an even greater problem because for those who have passed away, it can go undetected for years. We want to honor the memory of loved ones without letting their personal information get into the wrong hands. Be sure to follow these guidelines:

- Limit personal information in newspaper and online obituaries.
- Send a copy of the death certificate to each credit reporting agency and ask them for a "deceased alert" on the deceased's credit report.
- Notify the Social Security Administration of the death.
- Send the IRS a copy of the death certificate with a final tax return, if due.
- Continue to review the deceased's credit report for questionable credit card activity at least six months after the expiration dates.

The last thing you want is for your or a deceased loved one's credit card, account number, or Social Security number to end up on the Dark Web. Long after the funerals and memorials have ended, the steady syphoning of finances from the living could begin if these credentials are not safe and hidden away. Treat all digital activity the same way you did when the deceased were still alive. Do not follow or friend anyone you or they did not know. Do not frivolously subscribe to any services, regardless of what they promise. And always keep an eye on a deceased loved one's financial statements and accounts to ensure no one is stealing money or memories from those who rightfully deserve them.

Depending on a loved one's hobbies and interests, you may want to go that extra mile and delete all of their browser history. Also, after the estate settles, you might consider thinning out their physical files by shredding older documents containing sensitive information. I also recommend taking some time to decide where their digital storage devices should reside and whether they should be wiped clean and reused or sold. These considerations are especially pertinent if you decide to donate computers to Goodwill or some other charitable organization. The same holds true for USB sticks, external hard drives, printers, fax machines, scanners, and cellphones, as they all have capacity to store files in memory that could be snatched by a cybercriminal.

In the case of social media, many deceased users live on digitally in the form of memorial pages. Facebook, Instagram, Twitter, and Snapchat all offer memorialization of the deceased, but the companies also require a copy of the death certificate in order to officially close or transfer control to a partner or family. This requirement might seem extreme to some, but social media can play an even bigger role after someone has died than when they were alive. Many social media accounts posthumously collect donations and wield great influence over followers and friends, so legal and administrative control over those accounts is paramount for the surviving family or partner.

If this seems like too much to handle or think about, there are resources, such as www. thedigitalbeyond.com, for step-by-step planning before and after a loved one passes. And www. everplans.com provides expert guidance and services, allowing administrators to create and share all aspects of the deceased with family and friends in a secure and private manner for a yearly fee.

Important Contact Information:
Department of Veterans Affairs
1-800-827-1000
https://www.va.gov/

Social Security Administration
1-800-772-1213
https://www.ssa.gov/benefits/survivors/

Credit Reporting Agencies
EQUIFAX
1-800-685-1111
http://www.equifax.com/

TRANS UNION
1-800-888-4213
https://www.transunion.com/

EXPERIAN
1-888-397-3742
https://www.experian.com/

Afterword:
A Beautiful Mind

The original Senior Cyber, Bill Schober (right) stands
proudly next to his son Gary Schober (left).

George (Bill) Schober was born on September
24, 1919. He grew up in West Orange, New
Jersey, with his parents and two brothers. He
joined the US Navy soon after graduating high
school, where his knowledge of electronics
was put to use as the primary organizer of all
electronic equipment sent to the ships in the

Pacific Theater. When he left the navy, Bill returned to his family in New Jersey and got a job with Western Electric just before starting his own family. Bill Schober passed away on July 16, 2019. He was my grandfather and, next to my own father, was quite possibly the smartest man I will ever know.

As a young boy growing up during the Great Depression, Bill was fascinated with radio technology and quickly earned his amateur radioman license. This love of technology led to many significant contributions throughout his life, including the first broadcast television studio in the world, located in Clifton, New Jersey. Bill took it upon himself to devise a transmitter that would broadcast all the way from Passaic to the 1939 New York World's Fair in Flushing Meadows, where a state-of-the-art Dumont TV was on display. Disney learned of this transmitter operation and quickly provided cartoons for the studio to transmit and display. It was the first of many firsts Bill Schober had a hand in inventing, but his ingenuity had also been passed down from his father, his father's father, and even a legendary inventor.

Including me, there were actually five generations of Schobers working in technology, and all had brushes with greatness. Both Bill Schober's father and grandfather worked directly under the famous inventor and Wizard of Menlo Park, Thomas Edison. As a machinist in Edison's famed Menlo Park laboratory, located a stone's throw from Edison, New Jersey—where my mother and father raised my brother, sister, and me)—Bill's grandfather worked on the floor with hundreds of other skilled mechanics at the end of the nineteenth century. These skilled craftsmen oversaw the development of thousands of invention prototypes, ranging from Edison's exalted light bulb filaments to the first carbon button microphones used in early telephone handsets. Over four hundred patents for inventions originated in the Menlo Park laboratory until Edison moved operations about twenty miles north to West Orange, New Jersey.

Both my great-grandfather and his father worked for Edison into the early twentieth century, and even though my grandfather never spoke to us about that time in history, I cannot help but think it somehow instilled a great sense of curiosity and inspiration within him even though he hadn't even been born yet.

George H. Schober Sr. was my great-grandfather, and he was known for his practical jokes and ingenuity. I never met him but am told he was a particularly short man (most of his descendants were actually rather tall) with an equally short resume of formal education. In fact, he was kicked out of grammar school permanently for urinating on a radiator in his classroom as a prank. However, his lack of education did not prevent him from contributing greatly to emerging industries and innovation. Like his father, George H. Schober Sr. worked as a mechanic for Thomas Edison until Edison scooped him up as his personal chauffeur for a number of years. But George's first love was building and fixing machines, so he spent most of his later years fulfilling large orders for the aircraft industry. He developed machinery that could improve output even further by automatically indexing brass drilling bits to make airplane parts, all from his basement in West Orange, New Jersey. For a brief time, he even moved his machinery into the original building that launched Berkeley Varitronics Systems, Inc., the company that my father, Gary W. Schober, founded.

In January 1942, Bill Schober married the love of his life, Florence Ruh, and they had three children and a marriage lasting seventy-one years until her death in 2011. Since then, the Schober family has increased to eight grandchildren and fifteen great-grandchildren. My father, who served as such a great inspiration to my own understanding of electronics and wireless technology, grew up in the 1940s and '50s in Cranford, New Jersey, under a loving but reserved Schober household led by my grandfather Bill. He taught my father, Gary, everything he knew about radios but wasn't content as just an amateur radio license holder. Bill Schober was ready to move into the big leagues of technology before "big tech" was even a thing.

Bill Schober worked for Bell Labs for forty-two years during its golden age of innovation, making many critical contributions. In the early 1950s, Bill oversaw the development and testing of underseas cable that would carry telephone calls from New Jersey all the way to England. In the early 1960s, Bill and his Bell Labs team designed and built Telstar, the world's first communications satellite. In fact, they built five satellites and successfully launched two of them into space, where they were the first to reflect signals off the moon and onto Australia. All five satellites contained his name and W2OJ, his amateur radio operator (HAM) call letters.

Bill Schober continued to communicate with other HAMs around the world into his retirement but would now do so from his homes in

Berkeley Heights and Highland Lakes, New Jersey, where he spent his golden years with his ever-growing family.

When Bill and Florence Schober eventually moved to Cedar Crest, a retirement community located in northern New Jersey, he and a group of twelve other licensed radio operators were given space in the Village Square to set up their own radio station. Bill also kept enough of his own equipment to set up a station in his apartment and until his eyesight failed, he was the sound engineer for the Cedar Crest television station. Every morning at six o'clock, Bill joined his "Rooster Network." The fifty or so radiomen and women were from as far south as Florida and as far north as Canada, extending well into the Midwest.

My grandfather was always a quiet and dignified man. I have many fond childhood recollections of him, but when he wasn't bouncing his young grandchildren on his knee, the memories that best describe him usually involved him sitting by himself on his HAM rig, dialing in a distant voice and talking to someone on the other side of the world, never truly alone.

Until his final years, Bill Schober maintained a sharp mind, always tinkering and still inventing. After his wife passed, he never remarried or left New Jersey, so my parents became his part-time caretakers. My father would check in on him, helping him set up the latest iPad or computer so my grandfather could stay connected to the world through technology. It represented a new world for him, and he did his best, even trying to teach my own children how to use technology while staying safe. But as the years went on, he had difficulty seeing and using the little touchscreens filled with apps and icons, so we all pitched in to help.

One of the reasons I wrote this book was to help seniors who may not have the benefit of large and loving families or groups of friends to help navigate the world of new technology, which can sometimes be dangerous. My grandfather became the target of many phone and internet investment scams, and if left to his own devices, he could've easily given it all away to criminals. Fortunately, we were there to intercept bogus phone calls, throw out junk mail he might have responded to, and guide him through email correspondences that could've gone horribly wrong.

Bill Schober spent most of his adolescent and adult life communicating with others through HAM radio, a point-to-point medium. The internet and its vast network full of simultaneous users, messages, and platforms were somewhat lost on him. I suppose this kept him secure enough, but I also believe it hampered his quality of life, even as he approached the age of a centenarian.

His last years of life certainly weren't his best years, but during that time, he always maintained his dignity. I'd like to think modern technology helped him convey his needs and desires to those who couldn't be near him as often as they wanted. I hope his story inspires you to embrace technology while still maintaining a healthy knowledge of scammers, predators, and criminals. Whether you're launching satellites into space or just sending a text to a loved one, technology is always about communication and expression in the end. As long as you can stay safe while achieving this, you will always follow in the footsteps of Bill Schober, the original Senior Cyber.

Appendix: Senior Scams and What to Look For

This information will help you identify email scams quickly. Remember that the goals of the scammers can vary. Some scammers want to dupe you into sending them money. However, others simply want you to click on the obvious link in the email itself or open an attachment so harmful malware can be immediately downloaded to your computer.

Depending on the type of malware or destination of the URL link, a number of things can happen to your private data, including your passwords and account numbers:

- it can be taken and used in identity theft;
- your credit card information can be stolen and used for fraudulent purchases;
- your contacts can be harvested and sold to other scammers;
- as in the case of John Podesta, your private emails and other communications can be stolen and used to harm you or others (possible extortion); or
- your entire computer contents can be frozen until you pay the scammer/hacker a ransom to unlock it.

Note that these are just a few reasons to become aware of email scams and have a robust antivirus program like Avast that scans your computer in the background for the latest threats. And make sure it is constantly running the latest updated version.

Below are examples of some common email scams you might encounter.

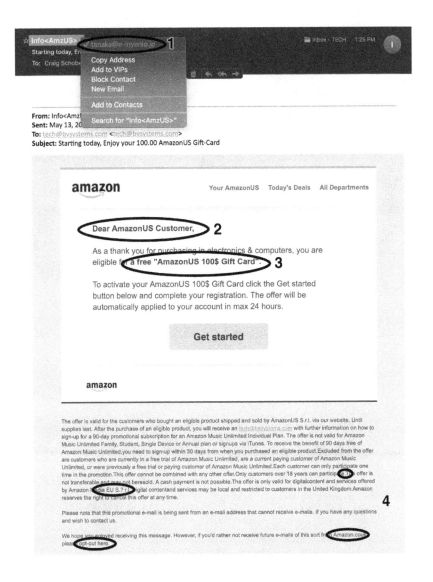

A SCAMMER PRETENDING TO BE AMAZON:

1. The "From" category of email scams can be deceiving. For example, it appears

that this email is from Amazon, but you can easily click on the sender's email name to see the actual sender's email address, which *should* be from Amazon. com. In this case, though, it looks like the email came from some scammer with an "e-invenio.jp" server domain. The ".jp" indicates the server is in Japan, even though the email references Amazon in both the United States and Great Britain.

2. If you have an Amazon account, you can be sure the company knows your full name and other important information. However, since scammers rarely know much (if anything) about you, they might address you as "AmazonUS Customer" because they don't know your real name.

3. Notice the syntax, spacing, bold type, and use of quotes in: **a free "AmazonUS 100$ Gift Card"**. This is sloppy and oddly phrased for a trillion-dollar company like Amazon with a professional marketing

department that sends out millions emails every single day; the real Amazon does not make these kinds of mistakes.

4. In the fine print at the bottom, notice all the tiny punctuation errors, lack of proper spacing, and missing links. The terms appear to match legitimate Amazon emails, but that's because the scammers simply copied and pasted bits from real Amazon emails. However, they neglected to assemble the bits back into a proper fashion, so it looks strange.

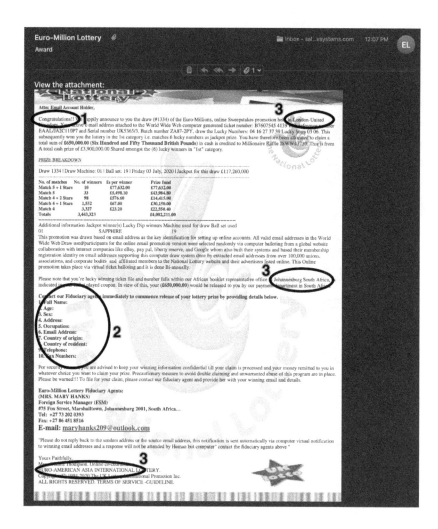

A SCAMMER PRETENDING TO BE A LOTTERY COMMISSION:

1. If you receive a congratulatory email for winning any kind of contest you did not enter, it is a scam—especially if it

appears to be from the "Euro Lottery," which doesn't even exist.

2. *Never reveal any personal information to any organization you do not know or trust.* Since there is no lottery and no prize, this scam email can generate revenue only by collecting as much information as possible and then selling it to other scammers. If you provide any information, expect to receive many more scam emails in the future.

3. This Euro Lottery email claims to originate in the United Kingdom. It mentions an office in Johannesburg, South Africa. It also references American Asia International Lottery as well. By trying to be as inclusive as possible, these scammers are casting a wide net to catch as many victims as possible around the world.

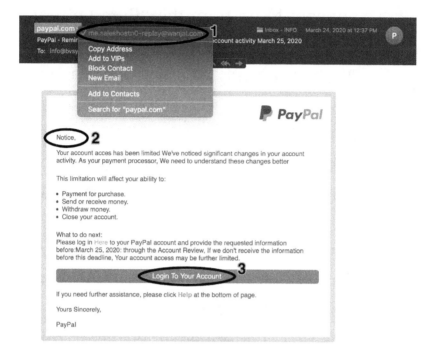

A SCAMMER PRETENDING TO BE PAYPAL:

1. This email looks like it came from PayPal, but it really came from "me. saleshostn0-replay@wanjai.com." There are millions of emails in circulation that spoof PayPal. If you receive any email that claims to be from PayPal and you are not sure, simply forward it to spoof@ paypal.com, and they will tell you whether it is legitimate or not.

2. Since PayPal knows the names and emails of all of its users, official emails would never address you as "Notice."

3. When the real PayPal includes buttons on the bottom of its emails, these buttons give a specific call to action, such as "Get the Details" or "Accept the Money." You should never click on any link in an email you were not expecting or you don't recognize, especially the supposed links for logging into an account.

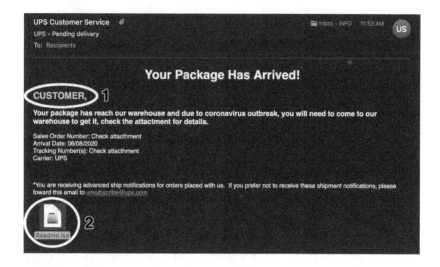

A SCAMMER PRETENDING TO BE UPS:

1. If you are a UPS customer, the company knows your name, address, and much more, so any legitimate communication from UPS will include your name.

2. Never click on any email attachments. "Readme.iso" is an executable file and is there only to install malware onto your computer. If you do click on it by mistake, simply close all pop-up windows and delete the email. Then run a scan with your antivirus software.

A SCAMMER PRETENDING TO BE NETFLIX:

1. If you glance at it quickly, "contact-membnetfloxme.info" might look like "contactmembnetflixme.info." While neither email address could be from Netflix, if the scammers can fool just one out of every one hundred thousand people, they are doing their jobs.

2. Scammers love to scare their victims into immediate action with ominous alerts and telling them their "account is on hold." Stop and think before you do anything. Is your Netflix working? Even if it's not working, that could easily be a coincidence. Log in to your Netflix account through the app or by typing the company's URL directly into your browser and check the status yourself.

3. Action buttons like these look like short-cuts to avoid unnecessary navigation to your Netflix account, but those buttons will not take you to the real Netflix website or your account. They will take you to a different website on a different server that is designed only to scrape (meaning steal) log-in credentials and sell them to the highest bidders. Always log in to your Netflix account the same way you have in the past, not by clicking a link in an email.

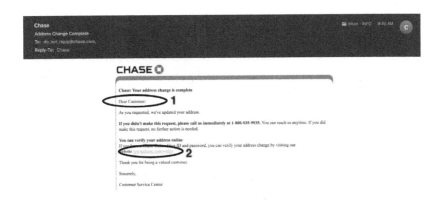

A SCAMMER PRETENDING TO BE CHASE BANK:

1. This looks like it could be a legitimate email from Chase Bank, but since I am not a Chase customer, I know it's more likely to be a scam than a mistake. If I were a Chase customer, though, I would know whether or not I made an address change. I could also simply log into my Chase account the same way I always do—without clicking on the link—and double-check any claims made in the email. And if I were a customer, Chase would know my name, so the "Dear Customer" is also a tipoff to a scam.

2. The URL www.chase.com/verify looks like a legitimate URL, but that doesn't

mean the link will take you to the indi-cated website. Any destination address can be assigned to any underlined URL as it appears. If you suspect the email is a scam or the address shown is not real, type it manually into your browser. If it is real, you will know soon enough, and if not, you just avoided a possible hack or scam.

Acknowledgments

The authors would like to thank the following people who helped make this book possible:

Gary Schober

Eileen Schober

Bill Schober

Ted Schober

Connell Rooney

Kelly Dwyer

Bill Dwyer

Every senior out there willing to try new technology, embrace the internet, and fight back against cybercriminals

All illustrations contained within this book were provided by Jake Thomas of www.JakeThomasCreative.com.

About the Authors

Scott N. Schober is the president and CEO of Berkeley Varitronics Systems (BVS), a forty-eight-year-old, family-owned company in New Jersey that designs and builds advanced wireless solutions and products for worldwide telecom and security markets. He is a cybersecurity and wireless technology expert, author, and host of a weekly video podcast entitled *What Keeps You Up At Night?* Scott's first book, *Hacked Again*, is a top-selling cybersecurity book and currently boasts over two hundred reviews (4.7 out of 5 star review average) on Amazon. *Hacked Again* chronicles his experiences as a hacking victim when BVS was hacked in 2013 and how he overcame those circumstances and shared his experiences to help others avoid being hacked. Scott's second book, *Cybersecurity*

Is Everybody's Business, was cowritten with his brother, Craig. In this industry-acclaimed book, the two authors focus on cybersecurity practices for small businesses and home offices that they have learned through years of running their own successful business.

Scott is a highly sought-after cybersecurity expert for media appearances on hundreds of news networks, including Bloomberg TV, *Good Morning America*, NPR, Bill O'Reilly, CNN, Fox Business Channel, CGTN, i24 News, News 12 NJ, and many more. Scott also regularly presents on cybersecurity best practices for small business and consumer protections at security conferences, including RSA, FutureCon, SecureWorld, ShowMeCon, and Cyber Investing Summit as a keynote speaker and panel expert. His expertise extends to such topics as the future of wireless technology, protection from insider threats, susceptibility to cyber breaches, the impact of drones, and distracted driving technology. You can learn more about him at www.ScottSchober.com.

Craig W. Schober is a writer, videographer, and the communications manager of Berkeley Varitronics Systems (BVS). In addition to his contributions to and edits of *Hacked Again* and *Cybersecurity Is Everybody's Business*, Craig creates all marketing content for BVS in the form of weekly blogs, white papers, website and e-commerce design and management, video podcasts, and viral video campaigns. Craig works closely with Scott as both a technical writer and video editor and has also worked in the film and video industry for the past twenty-five years, including as the writer, director, editor, and producer of his own award-winning feature films available on iTunes. He also happens to be Scott's younger brother.

Scott and Craig can both be contacted through www.bvsystems.com.

CPSIA information can be obtained
at www.ICGtesting.com
Printed in the USA
BVHW041922180121
598067BV00012B/43/J

9 780996 902298